WESTMAR COLLEGE LIBRARY

W9-BVH-186

Student Team Learning:

An Overview and Practical Guide

The Author

Robert E. Slavin is Director of the Elementary School Program, Center for Research on Elementary and Middle Schools, The Johns Hopkins University, Baltimore. He is also the author of *Cooperative Learning: Student Teams*, published by NEA.

The Advisory Panel

Cyndy Arras, Severely and Learning Handicapped Specialist, Margaret Keating School, Klamath, California

Olivia Besteiro, Resource Teacher, R. L. Martin Elementary School, Brownsville, Texas

James Boehlke, Guidance Counselor, Washington High School, Two Rivers, Wisconsin

Earl D. Clark, Associate Professor, School of Education, University of Alaska, Juneau

Jean H. Hayman, Director, Federally Funded Program for Disadvantaged Postsecondary Students, Alpena Community College, Michigan

Thomas W. Hine, sixth grade teacher, Wolcott School, West Hartford, Connecticut

Liz Kebric, Language Arts Department Head, Clear Lake Intermediate School, Houston, Texas

Beulah Priest-White, English instructor, Choppee High School, Georgetown, South Carolina

Denny L. Schillings, teacher, Homewood-Flossmoor High School, Flossmoor, Illinois

William G. Sears, retired elementary teacher, District 54, Schaumburg, Illinois

Student Team Learning:

An Overview and Practical Guide

SECOND EDITION

by Robert E. Slavin

National Education Association
Washington, D.C.

Copyright © 1988, 1986, 1983
National Education Association
of the United States

Note

The opinions expressed in this publication should not be construed as representing the policy or position of the National Education Association. Materials published by the NEA Professional Library are intended to be discussion documents for educators who are concerned with specialized interests of the profession.

Printing History
    First Printing: September 1983
    Second Printing: June 1986
    SECOND EDITION: June 1988
    Fourth Printing: October 1989

Acknowledgment

The drawings in this publication are the work of Charles Beady.

Library of Congress Cataloging-in-Publication Data

Slavin, Robert E.
  Student team learning.

  (Developments in classroom instruction)
  Bibliography: p.
  1. Group work in education.   2. Team learning
approach in education.   I. Title.   II. Series.
LB1032.S546   1988   371.3'95   88-12539
ISBN 0-8106-1836-2

Contents

Author's Preface
to the Second Edition

The Age of Cooperation is finally approaching in America's schools. Throughout the United States and in several other countries, teachers are enthusiastically learning and using cooperative learning methods at all grade levels and in all subjects.

In the years since the publication of the first edition of this monograph, there have been many advances in both research and development of cooperative learning methods. This Second Edition brings readers up to date on these developments, while maintaining a concise, practical presentation of guidelines for successful use of cooperative learning methods. It is adapted from *Using Student Team Learning* (22),* the original manual for the cooperative learning methods developed and researched at Johns Hopkins University.

The research and development that led to Student Team Learning dates back to 1970. Most of the funding for the research has come from the National Institute of Education (NIE), except for research on Student Team Learning and mainstreaming, which was funded by the U.S. Office of Special Education. Development of curriculum materials and dissemination have been supported by NIE, the National Diffusion Network, and the National Science Foundation.

The methods described in this book are not the work of any single individual. I am primarily responsible for Student Teams-Achievement Divisions (STAD) and, with Marshall Leavey and Nancy Madden, for Team Accelerated Instruction (TAI). Cooperative Integrated Reading and Composition (CIRC) was developed by Nancy Madden, Robert Stevens, and myself. I adapted Jigsaw II from work by Elliot Aronson. Teams-Games-Tournaments is primarily the creation of David DeVries and Keith Edwards. John Hollifield and Gail Fennessey have contributed to the writing of earlier training manuals, of which this book is a descendant. Charles Beady contributed the drawings to this publication.

The opinions expressed in this book are those of the author; they do not represent the policy of the U.S. Department of Education.

For information concerning any aspect of Student Team Learning, including how to obtain copies of the Teacher's Manual, curriculum materials, filmstrips, regional or local training workshops, the names of state facilitators of the National Diffusion Network, or other information, please contact

The Johns Hopkins Team Learning Project
Center for Social Organization of Schools
Johns Hopkins University
3505 North Charles Street
Baltimore, MD 21218
301-338-8249

*Numbers in parentheses appearing in the text refer to the Bibliography beginning on page 76.

Introduction

Do you remember being on a softball team, up at bat, with your teammates behind you shouting, "Hit it a mile!"? You knew you would do your best because your peers depended on you. The thrill of coming through for the team, of being the star even for a day, is one that few people forget. Being on a team, working for a cooperative goal, can be one of the most exciting experiences in life.

Can this kind of peer support for achievement, the easy acceptance of teammates, and the excitement of teamwork be transferred to the classroom? Such authors as James Coleman in *The Adolescent Society* (5) and Urie Bronfenbrenner in *Two Worlds of Childhood* (4) have suggested that teams could work in the classroom, and a long tradition of research in social psychology has shown that people working for a cooperative goal come to encourage one another to do their best, to help one another do well, and to like and respect one another (17). But how can team learning be made practical and effective in the classroom?

This question touched off fifteen years of research and development in classrooms. The result may be one answer to a major contemporary dilemma of schools: techniques that achieve both humanistic educational goals *and* basic skills learning goals instead of achieving one at the expense of the other.

When teachers place students on learning teams, each student knows that a group of peers supports his or her academic efforts. This is true because team success requires that all members do their best. Think back to the softball game. If you got that hit, your teammates went wild with approval; if you didn't, they consoled you and began encouraging the next batter. Can you remember anything like that happening in class? If you can, it was probably in a team spelling bee or other team activity in which your academic efforts could help a group achieve success.

TEAM TECHNIQUES

Educational research has demonstrated that heterogeneous teams made up of high and low achievers, boys and girls, Blacks, whites, and Hispanics, can be successfully transplanted from the playing field to the classroom. Several Student Team Learning techniques have now been extensively researched and found to significantly increase student learning. Some are designed for specific subjects and grade levels, and some are generic, broadly applicable methods. The latter, which are emphasized in this book, include Student Teams-Achievement Divisions, Teams-Games-Tournaments, and Jigsaw.

8

Student Teams-Achievement Divisions (STAD)

In STAD, the simplest of the Student Team Learning methods, students are assigned to four- or five-member learning teams. Made up of high-, average-, and low-performing students, boys and girls, students of different racial or ethnic backgrounds, each team is a microcosm of the entire class. Each week, the teacher introduces new material in a lecture or a discussion. Team members then study worksheets on the material. They may work problems one at a time in pairs, take turns quizzing each other, discuss problems as a group, or use whatever means they wish to master the material. The students also receive worksheet answer sheets, making clear to them that their task is to learn the concepts, not to simply fill out the worksheets. Team members are told they have not finished studying until all are sure they understand the material.

Following team practice, students take quizzes on the material they have been studying. Teammates may *not* help one another on the quizzes; they are on their own. The quizzes are scored in class or soon after; then the individual scores are formed into team scores by the teacher.

The amount each student contributes to his or her team is determined by the amount the student's quiz score exceeds his or her past quiz average. This improvement score system gives every student a good chance to contribute maximum points to the team if (and only if) the student does his or her best, and shows substantial improvement or completes a perfect paper. Use of improvement scores has been shown to increase student academic performance even without teams (23), but it is especially important as a component of Student Team Learning. Think back to the baseball game; the one problem in that sport is the automatic strikeout, the team member who cannot hit the ball no matter how much he or she practices. In Student Team Learning, no one is an automatic strikeout, and by the same token no one is guaranteed success, because it is improvement that counts.

A weekly one-page class newsletter recognizes the teams with the highest scores. The newsletter also recognizes the students who exceeded their own past records by the largest amounts or who completed perfect papers.

STAD is not difficult to use. Following the steps outlined in this book, teachers need only assign their students to teams, allow team members to study together, give a regular quiz, and do 30 to 40 minutes of team scoring at the end of the week. However, the change in the classroom is dramatic. Suddenly, students begin helping each other learn basic skills instead of resenting those who know the answers and making fun of those who do not. They begin to see the teacher as a resource person who has valuable information that they need to accomplish something important, more like a coach than a boss. They begin to see learning activities as social instead of isolated, fun instead of boring, under their own control instead of the teacher's. They begin to feel a camaraderie toward their classmates that is common on the athletic field but not in the classroom. In the integrated classroom, this new sense of camaraderie extends across racial or ethnic barriers to create new friendships less likely to exist in the traditional classroom. In the mainstreamed classroom, this camaraderie extends across an even larger barrier, that between physically or mentally handicapped students and their classmates, to create a climate of acceptance instead of scapegoating. Researchers have documented all these effects of Student Team Learning and many others (see the section on research evidence); what is so striking is that all these outcomes stem from the same simple change in classroom procedure.

Teams-Games-Tournaments (TGT)

Teams-Games-Tournaments uses the same teams, instructional format, and worksheets as STAD. In TGT, however, students play academic games to show their individual mastery of the subject matter. Students play these games in weekly tournaments in which they compete with members of other teams who are comparable in past performance. The competitions take place at tournament tables of three students. Thus, a high-performing student from the Fantastic Four might compete with a high performer from the Pirates and one from the Superstars. Another table might have average-performing students from the Pirates, the Masterminds, and the Chiefs, and another low performers from the Superstars, the Tigers, and the Masterminds. Of course, the students are not told which is the highest table, which is next, and so on, but they are told that their competition will always be fair. While teams stay together for about six weeks, the tournament table assignments change every week according to a system that maintains the equality of the competition. Equal competition makes it possible for students of all levels of past performance to contribute maximum points to their teams if they do their best, in the same way that the improvement score system in STAD makes it possible for everyone to be successful.

After the tournament, team scores are figured, and a newsletter recognizes the highest-scoring teams and tournament table winners. Thus TGT uses the same pattern of teaching, team worksheet study, individual assessment, equal opportunities for success, and team recognition as that used in STAD, but its use of academic games instead of quizzes makes TGT even more exciting and motivating than STAD. In fact, TGT generates so much excitement that getting students to stop can be a problem. For example, in one study in a Baltimore junior high school attended by a substantial number of students bused from the inner city, all the students in two classes stayed after school (and missed their buses) to attend a tie-breaker playoff in a TGT tournament. Teachers using TGT have reported that students never particularly interested in school were coming after class for materials to take home to study, asking for special help, and becoming active in class discussions.

Jigsaw

While STAD and TGT were developed at Johns Hopkins University, Jigsaw was originally designed by Elliot Aronson and his colleagues at the University of Texas and then at the University of California at Santa Cruz. In Aronson's Jigsaw method, students are assigned to six-member teams; academic material is broken down into five sections. For example, a biography may be divided into early life, first accomplishments, family life, major setbacks, and later life. First, each team member reads his or her unique section. If no students are absent, two students share a section. Next, members of different teams who have studied the same sections meet in ''expert groups'' to discuss their sections. Then, students return to their teams and take turns teaching their teammates about their sections. Since the only way students can learn about sections other than their own is to listen carefully to their teammates, they are motivated to support and show interest in each other's work.

This book emphasizes a modification of Jigsaw developed at Johns Hopkins University. In this method, called Jigsaw II, students work in four- to five-member teams as in TGT and STAD. Instead of each student having a unique section, all students read a common narrative, such as a book chapter, a short story, or a biography. However, each student receives a topic on which to become an expert. Students with the same topics meet in expert groups to discuss them, and return to their teams to teach their teammates what they have learned. Then students take individual quizzes, which are formed into team scores using the improvement score system of STAD, and a class newsletter recognizes the highest-scoring teams and individuals. Jigsaw II is easier to use than original Jigsaw because the teacher need not write separate readings for each topic.

For more information on Aronson's original Jigsaw method, see *The Jigsaw Classroom* (1).

Team Accelerated Instruction (TAI)

Team Accelerated Instruction is a combination of individualized instruction and team learning designed for use in elementary and middle school mathematics classes. In TAI, students work in the same heterogeneous teams as in the Student Team Learning methods (STAD, TGT, and Jigsaw II). However, in Student Team Learning, all students study the same materials at the same rate. In TAI, students are placed in individualized mathematics materials anywhere from addition to algebra, according to a placement test, and then work at their own levels and rates. Teammates check each other's work against answer sheets, except for final tests, which are scored by student monitors (who change each day). Team scores are based on the average number of units completed each week by the team members and the accuracy of the units; teams that meet a preset criterion receive attractive certificates or other rewards. The teams and the monitors manage all the routine checking, assignment, and materials-handling parts of the individualized program, freeing the teacher to work with individuals and homogeneous math groups. Because it is an individualized program, TAI is especially appropriate for use in heterogeneous math classes—such as those containing mainstreamed, low-achieving students and/or gifted students.

Cooperative Integrated Reading and Composition (CIRC)

The newest of the Student Team Learning methods is a comprehensive program for teaching reading and writing in the upper elementary grades (O).* In CIRC, teachers use basal readers and reading groups, much as in traditional reading programs. However, students are assigned to teams composed of pairs of students from two different reading groups. While the teacher is working with one reading group, students in the other groups are working in their pairs on a series of cognitively engaging activities, including reading to one another, making predictions about how narrative stories will come out, summarizing stories to one another, writing responses to stories, and practicing spelling, decoding, and vocabulary. Students work in teams to master main idea and other comprehension skills. During language arts periods, students engage in writing drafts, revising and editing one another's work, and preparing team or class books for publication.

---

*Letters in parentheses appearing in the text refer to the Additional Resources for the Second Edition beginning on page 78.

SIMILARITIES AND DIFFERENCES BETWEEN METHODS

STAD, TGT, and Jigsaw II share a score of features:

1. Four- to five-member, heterogeneous learning teams
2. Reward-for-improvement scoring (or equal competition)
3. Team recognition.

The weekly sequence of activities in these methods, however, is not the same. Figure 1 summarizes the basic schedule for each method.

The only difference between STAD and TGT comes after students have studied in their teams. In STAD, students take a quiz to show how much they have learned, and their team scores are based on the amount each team member has gained in achievement over his or her past record. The teaching and team study components of TGT are the same as in STAD, but instead of taking a quiz, students compete at ability-homogeneous tournament tables against representatives of other teams to show how much they have learned, and team scores are based on the team members' tournament points. In Jigsaw II, the initial information input is from textual materials instead of (or in addition to) teacher instruction. Each team member receives an expert topic. After reading, students discuss their topics in expert groups composed of all other students in the class who had the same topic. After the discussion, students report to their teams. Then, everyone is quizzed, and improvement points and team scores are computed as in STAD.

STUDENT TEAM LEARNING: THE RESEARCH EVIDENCE*

Achievement

For a teacher deciding whether or not to use a new instructional method, the first question is usually, "Will it increase my students' learning?"

In the case of Student Team Learning, the answer is, "Yes, in most cases." A total of forty studies of at least four weeks' duration have evaluated STAD, TGT, TAI, and CIRC. In all the studies, which took place in regular classrooms without aides or special resources, one of the Student Team Learning methods was compared to traditionally taught classes studying the same material. In thirty-three of the forty studies, the students in the Student Team Learning classes learned significantly more than those in the traditionally taught classes; in seven, there were no differences (25). In most of these studies, teachers or classes were randomly assigned to Student Team Learning or traditional methods, the treatments were used for at least six weeks, and care was taken to ensure that the traditionally taught classes had the same curriculum materials as the Student Team Learning classes. Such a high success rate in well-controlled studies is unusual in research on new 'instructional methods.

---

*For a more detailed review of the research, see *Cooperative Learning:Student Teams* (25).

Basic Schedule of Activities for STAD, TGT, and Jigsaw II

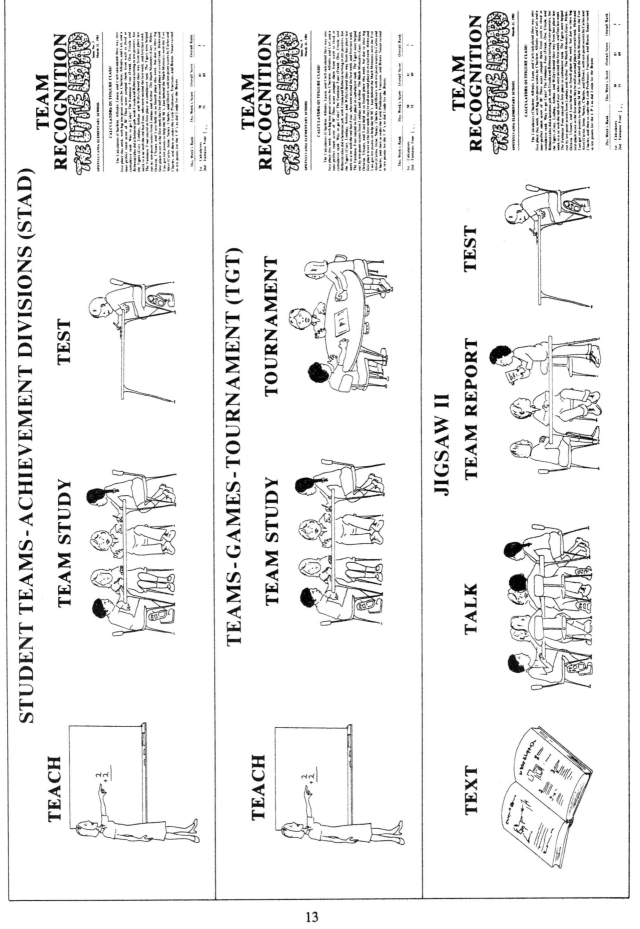

Figure 1

Student Teams-Achievement Divisions

STAD has been evaluated in twenty-one studies involving students in grades two through ten, in schools from inner-city Baltimore and Philadelphia to suburban Maryland to rural Maryland and Georgia to Nigeria, Israel, and West Germany. The subject areas have included language arts, mathematics, reading, science, and social studies. In sixteen of the studies, STAD was found to increase learning significantly more than traditional methods; in five there were no differences (20). STAD has been approved by the Joint Dissemination Review Panel, a U.S. Department of Education agency that examines research evidence on new programs and certifies for dissemination those that meet stringent requirements.

Teams-Games-Tournaments

TGT has been evaluated in nine studies in regular classrooms involving nearly 3,000 students in grades three to twelve. Like STAD, TGT has been studied in all kinds of schools in different parts of the United States. These studies have involved mathematics, language arts, social studies, and reading (19). In eight of the studies, TGT students learned significantly more than traditionally taught students; in the ninth, there were no differences. Based on this research evidence, TGT has been approved for dissemination by the Joint Dissemination Review Panel.

Team Accelerated Instruction

Some of the largest effects of Student Team Learning methods have been found in studies of TAI. Five of six studies found substantially greater learning of mathematics computations in TAI than in control classes, while one study found no differences (E). Across all six studies, the TAI classes gained an average of twice as many grade equivalents on standardized mathematics computations measures as traditionally taught control classes. For example, in one eighteen-week study in Wilmington, Delaware, the control group gained .61 grade equivalents in mathematics computations, while the TAI classes gained 1.65 grade equivalents (J). These experimental-control differences were still substantial (though smaller) a year after the students were in TAI. TAI has also been approved for dissemination by the Joint Dissemination Review Panel.

Cooperative Integrated Reading and Composition

Two studies of CIRC (O) found substantial positive effects of this method on standardized tests of reading comprehension, reading vocabulary, language expression, language mechanics, and spelling in comparison to traditional control groups. The CIRC classes gained thirty to seventy percent of a grade equivalent more than control classes on these measures in both studies. In addition, positive effects of CIRC were found on writing and on oral reading skills.

It seems safe to say that Student Team Learning usually has important positive effects on student achievement. Teachers can feel confident that if they use these methods as described in this book, students will learn at least as well as and probably better than they will with their usual methods.

Integrating the Desegregated Classroom

One of the most important effects of Student Team Learning is on friendships among students of different ethnic backgrounds in desegregated classes. Anyone who has spent much time in a desegregated secondary school knows that white students associate mostly with white students, Blacks with Blacks, Hispanics with Hispanics, and so on. This situation is always disappointing to those who hoped that widespread desegregation would lead to greatly increased contact, and thereby respect and liking, among students of different ethnic backgrounds. It should perhaps not be too surprising, however, since in most desegregated schools, Black, white, and Hispanic students come from separate neighborhoods, ride different buses, and often come from different elementary schools.

In several studies that did not use Student Team Learning, students in traditionally structured, racially mixed classes were asked to name their friends (10). When the question was repeated a semester later, the proportion of Black students who named whites as their friends and whites who named Blacks either stayed the same or decreased. Apparently, assigning Black and white students to the same classes does not by itself increase friendship across racial lines.

A Team Solution

Student Team Learning is an obvious solution to the problem of integrating the desegregated classroom. We know from decades of research that when people work together for a common goal, they gain in respect and liking for one another. When Student Team Learning techniques were applied in desegregated classrooms, that was the finding. In three studies, the number of friends of a different ethnic group named by TGT students increased far more than did those of control students (7). Three additional studies found STAD to have the same effect (18, 21, 28). In fact, in many of these studies, the Student Team Learning students began to choose their classmates as friends as if ethnicity were no barrier to friendship. This never happened in the control classes. Jigsaw II has also been found to improve relationships across ethnic group lines (11, 29). In one of the STAD studies, the positive effects on intergroup relations were found to be present nine months after the end of the study (21). Traditionally taught students named few students outside their own racial groups as friends on the followup questionnaire, but former STAD students had many friends of a different race. A Toronto study also found positive effects of Jigsaw II on cross-ethnic friendships five months after the conclusion of the study (29). The Joint Dissemination Review Panel has approved Student Team Learning as a whole (STAD, TGT, and Jigsaw II) for dissemination because of the effects of these methods on intergroup relations.

Mainstreaming

Although ethnicity is a major barrier to friendship, it is not as large as the barrier between physically or mentally handicapped children and their normal-progress peers. The mandate of Public Law 94-142 to place as many children as possible in regular classrooms has created an unprecedented opportunity for handicapped children to take their place in the mainstream of society. But it has also created enormous practical problems for classroom teachers and has often led to social rejection of the handicapped children.

15

Once again, Student Team Learning is an answer. In the Student Team Learning classroom, mainstreamed students are assigned to teams just as other students are. If these students are physically handicapped, their classmates come to value the contribution they make to the team, but more importantly they come to see them as important individuals, not just as handicapped persons. If the mainstreamed students are academically handicapped, their opportunity to contribute points to their teams for showing improvement (STAD and Jigsaw) or for succeeding in competition with others of similar performance levels (TGT) also makes these students valued by their teammates. The teamwork makes them part of the group instead of separate and different, and provides them with teammates who encourage and assist their academic progress.

The research on Student Team Learning and mainstreaming has focused on the academically handicapped student. One study used STAD to attempt to integrate students performing two years or more below the level of their peers into the social structure of the classroom. The use of STAD significantly reduced the degree to which the normal-progress students rejected their mainstreamed classmates, and increased the academic achievement and self-esteem of all students, mainstreamed as well as normal-progress (15). Team Accelerated Instruction, or TAI, combines individualized instruction with team learning in mathematics, offering students the academic benefits of material at their own level and the academic and social benefits of working in cooperating teams. Research on TAI has also found positive effects on the acceptance of mainstreamed students as well as on the achievement, self-esteem, and positive behavior of all students (27). Other research using cooperative teams has also shown significant improvements in relationships between mainstreamed academically handicapped students and their normal-progress peers (2, 6).

Perhaps the most important fact about Student Team Learning in classes containing mainstreamed students is that these techniques are not just good for these children, they are good for all children. They offer the teacher a chance to incorporate the mainstreamed children into the classroom social system and meet their individual needs while doing not just as well, but better, with their normal-progress peers.

Liking of Others and Self

One of the most important aspects of a child's personality is self-esteem. Many people have assumed that self-esteem is a relatively stable personal attribute that schools have little ability to change However, several researchers working on Student Team Learning techniques have found that teams do increase students' self-esteem. Students in Student Team Learning and TAI classes have been found to feel better about themselves than do students in traditional classes. These improvements in self-esteem have been found for TGT (8), for STAD (15), for Jigsaw (3), for the three methods combined (26), and for TAI (27). Why does this occur? First, it has been consistently found that TGT and STAD students report that they like others and feel liked by others more than control students do (25). Liking of others and feeling liked by others are obvious components of feeling worthwhile.

Second, it seems likely that students feel (and are) more successful in their school work when they work in teams. This could also lead to an increase in self-esteem. Whatever the reason, the effect of Student Team Learning on self-esteem may be particularly important for long-term effects on mental health.

16

Other Outcomes

In addition to student achievement, positive race relations, liking of others, and self-esteem, effects of Student Team Learning have been found on a variety of other important educational outcomes. Increased positive interaction among emotionally disturbed adolescents has been found in two studies of TGT (19, 13). Other positive effects include liking of school, peer norms in favor of doing well academically, student feelings of control over their own fate in school, and student cooperativeness and altruism (24). TGT (9) and STAD (20) have been found to have positive effects on students' time on task, a variable that is coming to take on increasing importance as educators become more concerned about instructional effectiveness. TAI has been found to improve students' classroom behavior, friendship behaviors, and self-confidence (27). The striking feature of this research is the breadth of outcomes associated with the various team learning methods. One method may improve student achievement, another race relations, a third student self-esteem. But how many educational methods can claim to have documented so many different effects in well-controlled field experiments in schools? Positive effects on all variables measured are not found in every Student Team Learning study, but negative effects are almost never found, and the ratio of significantly positive to equal findings on the major variables (achievement, race relations, self-esteem) is about three to one (25, 24).

Is Student Team Learning Practical?

Many educational innovations introduced in recent years have required enormous amounts of teacher training and/or money to implement. Fortunately, Student Team Learning techniques are quite simple. Thousands of teachers located in every state have used TGT, STAD, or Jigsaw with nothing more than a one-day workshop, a teacher's manual similar to this book, and available curriculum materials. Many have used these methods with the manual alone. Teachers can obtain curriculum materials for TGT, STAD, and CIRC in most elementary and secondary subjects, distributed at cost by the Johns Hopkins Team Learning Project (see the Preface for the address), or they can make their own materials. TAI-Mathematics is distributed by Mastery Education Corporation (85 Main Street, Watertown, MA 02172). Student Team Learning methods have been used in grades one through college (although mostly in grades two through twelve), in subjects ranging from math to science to social studies to English to foreign language, in every part of the United States and in several foreign countries. They have been used for purposes ranging from improving basic skills for average students, to bringing low-performing students up to grade level, to providing a richer experience for gifted students. They have often been used specifically to improve race relations, to make mainstreaming more effective, or just to help students become more excited about school. Not every teacher may feel comfortable using Student Team Learning, but most who do are enthusiastic, and many report dramatic differences in their own feelings about teaching.

As noted earlier, STAD, TGT, and TAI are certified by the U.S. Department of Education's Joint Dissemination Review Panel (JDRP) for their effects on basic skills, and the entire Student Team Learning program is certified by the JDRP for effects on intergroup relations. This means that these programs are eligible for dissemination by the National Diffusion Network, which has a system of state facilitators in every state who help school districts adopt JDRP-approved programs.

Student Team Learning: A Practical Guide

WHICH METHOD SHOULD YOU USE?

No single instructional method can be used in all subject areas and for all purposes equally well; Student Team Learning is no exception. However, there are different methods based on cooperative, heterogeneous teams for almost all instructional circumstances. STAD and TGT can be used to teach any material in which questions with one right answer can be posed. This includes most material taught in mathematics, language arts, science, foreign language, and some parts of social studies, such as geography, graph or map skills, and any knowledge-level objectives. Jigsaw II is used most often in social studies, but it can also be applied to literature or parts of science in which students learn from narrative materials. The use of TAI is restricted to mathematics in grades two through eight; it is most needed in heterogeneous math classes, where all students should not be taught the same materials at the same rate. CIRC is restricted to reading, writing, and language arts instruction in grades two through six. Besides subject matter, there are other reasons teachers may choose one Student Team Learning method over another. Figure 2 summarizes the advantages and most appropriate subjects for STAD, TGT, Jigsaw II, TAI, and CIRC. Before deciding on a method, it will be helpful to read the overviews for each method that follow.

STUDENT TEAMS-ACHIEVEMENT DIVISIONS (STAD)

Overview

STAD is made up of five major components: class presentations, teams, quizzes, individual improvement scores, and team recognition. Descriptions of these components follow.

Class Presentations

The teacher initially introduces the material in a class presentation. In most cases, this is a lecture/discussion, but it can include an audiovisual presentation. Class presentations in STAD differ from usual teaching only in that they must clearly focus on the STAD unit. Thus, students realize that they must pay careful attention during the presentation, because doing so will help them do well on the quizzes, and their quiz scores determine their team scores.

Teams

Teams are composed of four or five students who represent a cross-section of the class in academic performance, sex, and race or ethnicity. The major function of the team is to prepare its members to do well on the quizzes. After the teacher

18

User's Guide to Student Team Learning

STAD

Use in Grades 2–12 in
- Mathematics.
- Language Arts.
- Science.
- Social Studies skills, such as geography, graph reading.
- Foreign language.
- Any material with single right answers.

Advantages:
- Frequent quizzes give feedback to students and teacher.
- Relatively quiet, businesslike form of Student Team Learning.
- Improvement scores challenge students.
- Takes less instructional time than TGT.
- Curriculum materials available in most subjects.

TGT

Use in Grades 2–12 in
- Mathematics.
- Language Arts.
- Science.
- Social Studies skills, such as geography, graph reading.
- Foreign language.
- Any material with single right answers.

Advantages:
- Students enjoy tournaments.
- Fair competition challenges students.
- Students do most scoring.
- Curriculum materials available in most subjects.

Jigsaw II

Use in Grades 3–12 in
- Social Studies, when students are learning from books or other readings.
- Literature.
- Science.
- Any material when information comes from books or other readings.

Advantages:
- Can be used for more open-ended objectives.
- Students take real responsibility for teaching teammates.
- Students exercise reading, teaching, discussing, and listening skills.
- Frequent quizzes give feedback to students and teacher.
- Improvement scores challenge students.
- Easily adapted to library research projects.

TAI

Use in Grades 2–8 in
- Mathematics.

Advantages:
- Individualization provides for needs of all students, gives students success at their own level.
- Students do almost all scoring and manage materials.
- Materials are completely prepared; very little out-of-class time needed.
- Materials cover skills from addition to algebra.
- Students usually learn math skills rapidly.

CIRC

Use in Grades 2–6 in
- Reading.
- Writing.
- Language Arts.

Advantages:
- Combination of mixed-ability teams and same-ability reading groups allows students to succeed at their own levels.
- Reading program replaces workbooks with engaging activities supported by reading research.
- Writing program provides practical approach to the writing process that combines writing and language arts instruction.

Figure 2

presents the material, the team meets to study worksheets or other material. The worksheets may be materials obtained from the Johns Hopkins Team Learning Project, or they may be teacher-made. Most often, the study takes the form of students quizzing one another to be sure that they understand the content, or working problems together and correcting any misconceptions if teammates make mistakes.

The team is the most important feature of STAD. At every point, the emphasis is on the members doing their best for the team, and on the team doing its best for its members. The team provides the peer support for academic performance that is important for effects on learning; it also provides the mutual concern and respect that are important for effects on such outcomes as intergroup relations, self-esteem, and acceptance of mainstreamed students.

Quizzes

After one to two periods of teacher presentation and one to two periods of team practice, students take individual quizzes composed of course content-relevant questions. The quizzes are designed to test the knowledge the students have gained from class presentations and team practice. During the quizzes students are not permitted to help one another. This ensures that every student is individually responsible for knowing the material.

Individual Improvement Scores

The idea behind the individual improvement scores is to give each student a performance goal that he or she can reach, but only by working harder than in the past. Any student can contribute maximum points to his or her team in this scoring system, but no student can do so without showing definite improvement over past performance. Each student is given a "base" score, the minimum score to achieve on each quiz. Then students earn points for their teams based on the amount their quiz scores exceed their base scores. After every two quizzes, base scores are recomputed—to challenge students who start performing better to improve further, and to adjust to a more realistic level the base scores that were set too high for other students.

Team Recognition

A newsletter is the primary means of rewarding teams and individual students for their performance. Each week, the teacher prepares a newsletter to announce team scores. The newsletter also recognizes individuals showing the greatest improvement or completing perfect papers, and reports cumulative team standings. In addition to or instead of the newsletter, many teachers use bulletin boards, special privileges, small prizes, or other rewards to emphasize the idea that doing well as a team is important.

Preparing to USE STAD

Materials

STAD can be used with curriculum materials specifically designed for Student Team Learning and distributed by the Johns Hopkins Team Learning Project, or it can be used with teacher-made materials. As of this writing, Johns Hopkins materials are available in the following areas: Mathematics for grades two through eight, High School Consumer Mathematics, Algebra I, and Geometry; Elementary and Junior High School Language Arts; Elementary and Secondary Nutrition; and Junior High School Life Science, Physical Science, and U.S. History. To obtain more information on these materials, write to the address given in the Preface.

It is quite easy for teachers to make their own materials, however. Simply make a worksheet, a worksheet answer sheet, and a quiz for each unit planned. Each unit should take three to five days of instruction. The individual improvement score system is based on 30-item quizzes, the length of the quizzes in the Johns Hopkins Team Learning materials. For this reason, it is best to include in the quizzes a total number of items that divide evenly into 30, such as 10, 15, or 30. See Appendix 3 for instructions for making curriculum materials for STAD.

Assigning Students to Teams

A team in Student Team Learning is a group of four or five students who represent a cross-section of the class in past performance, race or ethnicity, and sex. That is, a four-person team in a class that is one-half male, one-half female, three-quarters white, and one-quarter minority would have two boys and two girls and three white students and one minority student. The team would also have a high performer, a lower performer, and two average performers. Of course, "high performer" is a relative term; it means high for the class, not high compared to national norms.

Teachers assign students to teams, rather than letting students choose teams themselves, because students tend to choose others like themselves. Teachers take likes, dislikes, and "deadly combinations" of students into account in the assignment, but do not let students choose their own teams. Instead they follow these steps:

1. Make copies of Team Summary Sheets and Quiz Score Sheets. Before assigning students to teams, make one copy of a Team Summary Sheet for every four students in the class and one copy of a Quiz Score Sheet for every two weeks that STAD will be used. These forms can be copied from Appendix 5.

2. Rank students. On a sheet of paper, rank students in the class from highest to lowest in past performance. Use whatever information is available—test scores, grades, teacher judgment. If exact ranking is difficult, do the best you can.

3. Decide on the number of teams. Each team should have four members if possible. To decide on the number of teams, divide the number of students in the class by four. If the division is even, the quotient will be the number of four-member teams to have. For example, a class of 32 students will have eight teams with four members each. If the division is uneven, the remainder will be one, two, or three. Thus there will be one, two, or three teams composed of five members. For example, a class of 30 students will have seven teams—five with four members and two with five members.

4. Assign students to teams. When assigning students to teams, balance the teams so that (1) each team is composed of students whose performance levels range from low to average to high, and (2) the average performance level of all the teams in the class is about equal. There are two reasons for this: (1) students with different performance levels within a team can tutor each other; (2) by providing balanced teams, no single team has an advantage in academic performance. To assign students to teams, use the list of students ranked by performance. Assign team letters to each student. For example, in an eight-team class use the letters A through H. Start at the top of the list with the letter A; continue lettering toward the middle. Then, after using the last team letter, continue the lettering in the opposite order. For example, if you were using the letters A-H (as in Figure 3), assign the eighth and ninth students to Team H, the tenth to Team G, the next to Team F, and so on. When you reach the letter A stop and repeat the process from the bottom up, again starting and ending with the letter A.

Assigning Students to Teams

	Rank Order	Team Name
High-Performing Students	1	A
	2	B
	3	C
	4	D
	5	E
	6	F
	7	G
	8	H
Average-Performing Students	9	H
	10	G
	11	F
	12	E
	13	D
	14	C
	15	B
	16	A
	17	
	18	
	19	A
	20	B
	21	C
	22	D
	23	E
	24	F
	25	G
	26	H
Low-Performing Students	27	H
	28	G
	29	F
	30	E
	31	D
	32	C
	33	B
	34	A

Figure 3

22

Notice that two students in Figure 3 (17 and 18) are not assigned at this point. They will be added to teams as fifth members, but first the teams should be checked for race or ethnicity and sex balance. If, for example, one-fourth of the class is Black, approximately one student on each team should be Black. If the class has more than two major ethnic groups, assign students to teams to represent their proportion in the class. If the teams you have made based on performance ranking are not evenly divided on both ethnicity and sex (they will rarely be balanced on the first try), change the assignments by trading students of the same approximate performance level, but of different ethnicity or sex, between teams until there is a balance.

5. *Fill out Team Summary Sheets.* After assigning all students to teams, fill in the names of the students on each team on the Team Summary Sheets, leaving the team name blank.

If there are six or more teams, divide them into two leagues. Many teachers name the two leagues (e.g., American and National).

Determining Initial Base Scores

In addition to assigning students to teams, it is necessary to determine the initial base score for each student. A base score is the minimum the teacher expects the student to make on a 30-item quiz. Refer to the ranked list of students used to make team assignments. If the class has 25 or more students, give the first three students an initial base score of 20; the next three, 19; the next three, 18; and so on until you have assigned each student an initial base score. Put the base scores on a Quiz Score Sheet. If the class has 24 or fewer students, give the first two students an initial base score of 20; the next two, 19; and so on. Note that these base scores are just a start; they will be modified to reflect students' actual scores after every two quizzes. When these adjustments are made, the base score will eventually be set approximately five points below the student's average past quiz scores. If there are students at the very bottom of the list who the teacher feels have little chance of making even their base scores, their base scores should be set a little lower according to teacher judgment. Don't worry about setting base scores exactly; they will adjust themselves over time.

How to Start STAD

Start with the schedule of activities described in the following section. After teaching the lesson, announce team assignments and have students move their desks together to make team tables. Tell students that they will be working in teams for several weeks and competing for recognition in a class newsletter.

The first week of STAD is the hardest, but by the second week most students will settle into the pattern. Some students may complain about the teams to which they were assigned, but by the second week almost all such students find a way to get along with their teammates. Do not change team assignments after announcing them except under extreme circumstances, because it is students' realization that they will be in their team for several weeks that motivates them to work on getting along with their teammates instead of complaining about them.

Schedule of Activities

STAD consists of a regular cycle of instructional activities, as follows:

Teach—Present the lesson.

Team Study—Students work on worksheets in their teams to master the material.

Test—Students take individual quizzes.

Team Recognition—Compute team scores based on team members' improvement scores, and recognize high-scoring teams in a class newsletter or bulletin board.

These activities are described in detail in the following pages.

TEACH

Time: One to two class periods
Main Idea: Present the lesson
Materials Needed: Lesson plan

Each lesson in STAD begins with a class presentation. A filmstrip or movie or other technique can be used to introduce the lesson, but most teachers simply give a lecture/discussion. In the lesson, stress the following (adapted from Good and Grouws [12]):

- *Briefly review* any prerequisite skills or information.
- Stick close to the *objectives* that you will test.
- Focus on *meaning*, not memorization.
- Actively *demonstrate* concepts or skills, using visual aids and many examples.
- Frequently *assess* student comprehension by asking many questions..
- Have all students *work problems* or *prepare answers* to your questions.
- Call on students *at random* so that they will never know whom you may ask a question—this makes all students prepare themselves to answer. *Do not* just call on students who raise their hands.
- *Do not give long class assignments* at this point—have students work one or two problems or prepare one or two answers, then give them feedback.
- Always *explain why* an answer is correct or incorrect unless it is obvious.
- *Move rapidly* from concept to concept as soon as students have grasped the main idea.
- *Maintain momentum* by eliminating interruptions, asking many questions, and moving rapidly through the lesson.

TEAM STUDY

Time: One to two class periods
Main Idea: Students study worksheets in their teams.
Materials Needed:
- Two *worksheets* for every *team*
- *Two answer sheets* for every *team*

During team study, the team members' tasks are to master the material presented in the lesson and to help their teammates master the material. Students have worksheets and answer sheets they can use to practice the skill being taught and to assess themselves and their teammates. Each team receives only two copies of the worksheets and answer sheets to force teammates to work together, but if some students prefer to work alone or want their own copies, make additional copies available. During team study:

- Have teammates move their desks together or move to team tables.
- *Hand out worksheets* and answer sheets (two of each per team) with a minimum of fuss.
- Tell students to *work together in pairs or threes*. If they are working problems (as in math), each student in a pair or three should work the problem and then check with his or her partner(s). If anyone missed a question, his or her teammates have a responsibility to explain it. Students who are working on short-answer questions may quiz each other, with partners taking turns holding the answer sheet or attempting to answer the questions.
- Emphasize to students that they have not finished studying until they are sure their *teammates will make 100%* on the quiz.
- Make sure that students understand that the worksheets are for *studying*—not for filling out and handing in. For this reason it is important that students have the answer sheets to check themselves and their teammates as they study.
- Have students *explain* answers to each other instead of just checking each other against the answer sheet.
- When students have questions, have them *ask a teammate* before asking the teacher.
- While students are working in teams, *circulate through the class*, praising teams that are working well, sitting in with each team to hear how it is doing, and so on.

TEST

Time: One-half to one class period
Main Idea: Individual quiz
Materials Needed: One quiz per student

- Distribute the quiz and give students adequate time to complete it. *Do not let students work together on the quiz*; at this point they must show what they have learned as individuals. Have students move their desks apart if possible.
- Either allow students to *exchange papers* with members of other teams, or *collect the quizzes* to score after class. Be sure to have the quizzes scored and team scores figured in time for the next class if at all possible.

TEAM RECOGNITION

Main Idea: Figure individual improvement scores, team scores, and prepare a class newsletter or bulletin board.

Figuring Individual and Team Scores

As soon as possible after each quiz, figure individual improvement scores and team scores and write a class newsletter (or prepare a class bulletin board) to announce the team scores. If at all possible, announce the team scores in the first period after the quiz. This makes the connection between doing well and receiving recognition clear to students, which increases their motivation to do their best.

Improvement Points

The points that students earn for their teams are the differences between their quiz scores and their base scores. (See p. 23 for setting initial base scores.) Note that this system is based on 30-item quizzes, which are used in all the Johns Hopkins Team Learning materials. Teachers using their own quizzes, or dividing one of the Johns Hopkins quizzes into two or more shorter ones, must adjust scores to equal those of a 30-item quiz. For example, each item on a 10-item quiz is worth 3 points, each item on a 15-item quiz is worth 2 points, and each item on a 20-item quiz is worth 1½ points. Students can earn a maximum of 10 improvement points, and they receive the 10-point maximum for a perfect paper, regardless of their base score. The purpose of the maximum is to avoid putting an unfair ceiling on the possible scores of high-performing students. The minimum number of improvement points that students can earn is 0 (even if their quiz scores are below their base). Thus, a column of the Quiz Score Sheet could be filled out as shown in Figure 4.

Example of Base Scores and Improvement Points
Date: October 25
Quiz: Adding two digits without renaming

Student	Base Score	Quiz Score	Improvement Points
John	16	23	7
Mary	18	30	10
Tanya	23	30	10
Sam	16	27	10
Cheryl	17	17	0
Jose	21	23	2
Frank	18	17	0

Figure 4

Note that the improvement points are simply the difference between the quiz score and the base score, with a few exceptions. Mary and Sam would have earned more than 10 improvement points, but 10 is the maximum. Frank did not even make his base score, but he does not get negative improvement points—just 0. Figuring improvement points is not at all difficult, and with a little practice, it takes only a few minutes. The purpose of base scores and improvement points is to enable all students to bring maximum points to their teams, whatever their level of past performance. Students understand that it is fair that each one should be compared with his or her own level of past performance, as all students enter class with different levels of skills and experience in the subject.

Place the points you have calculated on each student's quiz—for example, Base Score = 18; Quiz Score = 23; Improvement Points = 5.

Team Scores

To figure team scores, enter each student's improvement points on the appropriate Team Summary Sheet. For four-member teams, simply add the individual improvement points to find the team scores; for two-, three-, or five-member teams, however, use Appendix 1 to prorate the total team scores to be comparable with those of the four-member teams. For example, if a five-member team had a total score of 25, its transformed score would be 20. Consider only the transformed score in determining the team standing and computing the cumulative score. Figure 5 shows two STAD team score sheets. Note that in the four-member team (Fantastic Four), the scores were simply added to find the total team score; in the five-member team (Five Alive), the score was prorated using Appendix 1.

Recognizing Team Accomplishments

Newsletters

As soon as possible after calculating each student's points and figuring team scores, write a newsletter to recognize successful teams. Newsletters can be written on one ditto master and class copies run off. In the newsletter, emphasize team success as much as possible. For example, mention students who received maximum scores (10 points), but always mention their teams. It is important to help students value team success. The teacher's own enthusiasm about team scores will help. If students take more than one quiz in a week, combine the quiz results into a single weekly newsletter report. Figure 6 shows a sample STAD newsletter. Note that the score of the five-member Five Alive team is represented with the total score, a slash, and the transformed score.

Bulletin Boards

Instead of or in addition to newsletters, bulletin boards may be used to recognize team success. Many teachers write the team names on strips of construction paper or poster board and display them in order of team standings on the last quiz. For example, one teacher put the team names on kites and arranged them so that the highest team was the highest kite; another put the team names on pictures of flowers and used the height of the flower to represent the team standing.

Other Rewards

The amount and kind of reward teachers give for team success will help determine the success of STAD, but different classes need different amounts or kinds. In many schools, especially those that have many students with motivation problems, it may be crucial to give the winning teams something more than (or instead of) the newsletter. For the top three teams, it could be refreshments, free time during class to play quiet board games or read, ribbons or trophies, permission to line up first for recess or to go to the next class, or some other inexpensive reward of value to students. The rewards need not be large to be quite important in convincing students that the teacher really values team success, although teacher attitude toward cooperation and team success will be more important than any amount of team reward.

Returning the First Set of Quizzes

When students receive the first set of quizzes with base scores, quiz scores, and improvement points, they will need an explanation of the improvement point system. This explanation should emphasize the following:

Examples of STAD Team Scores
TEAM SUMMARY SHEET

Figure 3. Examples of STAD Team Scores

TEAM SUMMARY SHEET

Team Name _Fantastic Four_

Team Members	1	2	3	4	5	6	7	8	9	10
Frank	8	10	8							
Otis	10	7	6							
Ursula	0	3	10							
Rebecca	7	10	10							
Total Team Score	25	30	34							
Transformed Team Score	—	—	—							
Team Standing This Week	2	1	2							
Cumulative Score	25	55	89							
Cumulative Standing	2	1	1							

TEAM SUMMARY SHEET

Team Name _The Five Alive_

Team Members	1	2	3	4	5	6	7	8	9	10
Carlos	10	5	10							
Ilene	6	1	4							
Nancy	10	10	6							
Charles	4	5	10							
Oliver	0	4	7							
Total Team Score	30	25	37							
Transformed Team Score	24	20	30							
Team Standing This Week	5	7	5							
Cumulative Score	24	44	74							
Cumulative Standing	5	6	5							

Figure 5

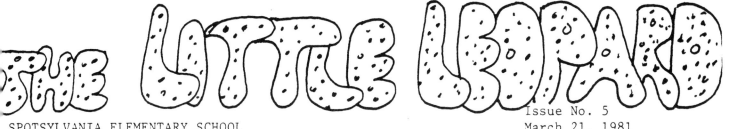

SPOTSYLVANIA ELEMENTARY SCHOOL

Issue No. 5
March 21, 1981

CALCULATORS OUTFIGURE CLASS!

The Calculators (Charlene, Alfredo, Laura, and Carl) calculated their way into first place this week, with big ten-point scores by Charlene, Alfredo, and Carl, and a near-perfect team score of 38! Their score jumped them from sixth to third in cumulative rank. Way to go Calcs! The Fantastic Four (Frank, Otis, Ursula, and Rebecca) also did a fantastic job, with Ursula and Rebecca turning in ten-pointers, but the Tigers (Cissy, Lindsay, Arthur, and Willy) clawed their way from last place last week to a tie with the red-hot Four, who were second the first week, and first last week. The Fantastic Four stayed in first place in cumulative rank. The Tigers were helped out by ten-point scores from Lindsay and Arthur. The Math Monsters (Gary, Helen, Octavia, Ulysses, and Luis) held on to fourth place this week, but due to their big first-place score in the first week they're still in second place in overall rank. Helen and Luis got ten points to help the M.M.'s. Just behind the Math Monsters were the Five Alive (Carlos, Irene, Nancy, Charles, and Oliver), with ten point scores by Carlos and Charles, and then in order the Little Professors, Fractions, and Brains. Susan turned in ten points for the L.P.'s as did Linda for the Brains.

- -

This Week's Rank	This Week's Score	Overall Score	Overall Rank
1st - Calculators	38	81	3
2nd - Fantastic Four ⟩ Tie	35	89	1
2nd - Tigers	35	73	6
4th - Math Monsters	40/32	85	2
5th - Five Alive	37/30	74	5
6th - Little Professors	26	70	8
7th - Fractions	23	78	4
8th - Brains	22	71	7

- -

TEN POINT SCORERS

Charlene	(Calculators)	Helen	(Math Monsters)
Alfredo	(Calculators)	Luis	(Math Monsters)
Carl	(Calculators)	Carlos	(Five Alive)
Ursula	(Fantastic Four)	Charles	(Five Alive)
Rebecca	(Fantastic Four)	Susan	(Little Professors)
Lindsay	(Tigers)	Linda	(Brains)
Arthur	(Tigers)		

Figure 6

29

1. The main purpose of the improvement point system is to give everyone a minimum score to try to beat and to set that minimum score based on past performance so that all students will have an equal chance to be successful if they do their best academically.
2. The second purpose of the improvement point system is to make students realize that the scores of everyone on their team are important—that all team members can earn maximum improvement points if they do their best.
3. The improvement point system is fair because everyone is competing only with himself or herself—trying to improve individual performance—regardless of what the rest of the class does.

Recomputing Base Scores after Two Quizzes

The initial assignment of base scores is just a beginning point. After the first two quizzes, it will be necessary to use Appendix 2 to determine each student's new base score. To do this, add each student's two quiz scores, and find the total score in the left-hand column of the table. Then find the old base score at the top of the table. Follow the row across and the column down to the point where they intersect. This will be the student's new base score. For example, suppose a student had a base score of 18 and quiz scores of 23 and 28, making a total quiz score of 51. Looking at Appendix 2, first find the number 51. Looking at Appendix 2, first find the number 51 in the left-hand column of the table. Then find the old base score (18) along the top of the table. At the intersection of this row and column is the number 20, which is the student's new base score. If a student has missed a quiz, double the one quiz score that is available and then use the table in the same way. If the student has missed both quizzes, give the student the old base score again. If a student receives a zero for skipping class or for some disciplinary reason, be sure to count it as a missed quiz for the purpose of assigning base scores.

Students should know their own base scores, but not those of other students. They should learn their base scores on a returned quiz or in some other private way.

Changing Teams

After five or six weeks of STAD, reassign students to new teams. This gives those who were on low-scoring teams a new chance, allows all students to work with other classmates, and keeps the program fresh.

Combining STAD with Other Activities

STAD may be used for part of the instruction, and other methods for other parts. For example, many English teachers use STAD three periods each week to teach language mechanics and usage, but they teach literature and writing the two remaining periods using other methods. STAD may also be used in combination with TGT or Jigsaw II.

Grading

Report card grades should be based on the students' actual quiz scores, not on improvement points or team scores. However, students' improvement points and/or team scores can be made a small part of their grades; or, if the school gives separate grades for effort, these scores can be used to determine the effort grades.

TEAMS-GAMES-TOURNAMENTS (TGT)

Overview

TGT is the same as STAD in every respect but one: instead of the quizzes and the individual improvement score system, TGT uses academic game tournaments, in which students compete as representatives of their teams with members of other teams who are like them in past academic performance. A description of the components of TGT follows.

Class Presentations

Same as for STAD.

Teams

Same as for STAD.

Games

The games are composed of simple, course content-relevant questions that students must answer, and are designed to test the knowledge students gain from class presentations and team practice. Games are played at tables of three students, each of whom represents a different team. Most games are simply numbered questions on a ditto sheet. A student picks a number card and attempts to answer the question corresponding to the number. A challenge rule permits players to challenge each other's answers.

Tournaments

The tournament is the structure in which the games take place. It is usually held at the end of the week, after the teacher has made a class presentation and the teams have had time to practice with the worksheets. For the first tournaments, the teacher assigns students to tournament tables—assigning the top three students in past performance to Table 1, the next three to Table 2, and so on. This equal competition, like the individual improvement score system in STAD, makes it possible for students of all levels of past performance to contribute maximally to their team scores if they do their best. Figure 7 illustrates the relationship between heterogeneous teams and homogeneous tournament tables. After the first week, however, students change tables depending on their own performance in the most recent tournament. The winner at each table is "bumped up" to the next higher table (e.g., from Table 6 to Table 5), the second scorer stays at the same table, and the low scorer is "bumped down." In this way, if students have been misassigned at first, they will eventually be moved up or down until they reach their true level of performance.

Team Recognition

Same as for STAD.

Assignment to Tournament Tables (TGT)

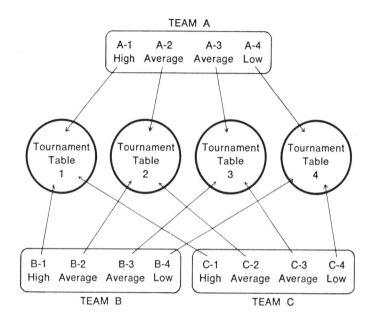

Figure 7

Preparing to Use TGT

Materials

Curriculum materials for TGT are the same as for STAD (see pp. 20–21). Also needed will be one set of cards numbered from 1 to 30 for every three students in the largest class. Teachers can obtain these from the Johns Hopkins Team Learning Project (see the Preface), or they can make their own by numbering colored index cards.

Assigning Students to Teams

Assign students to four- or five-member heterogeneous teams exactly as for STAD (see pp. 21–23).

Assigning Students to Initial Tournament Tables

Make a copy of the Tournament Table Assignment Sheet from Appendix 5. On it, list students from top to bottom in past performance in the same ranking used to form teams. Count the number of students in the class. If the number is divisible by three, all tournament tables will have three members; assign the first three students on the list to Table 1, the next three to Table 2, and so on. If the division has a remainder, one or two of the top tournament tables will have four members. For example, a class of 29 students will have nine tournament tables, two of which will have four members (29 ÷ 3 = 9 r 2). The first four students on the ranked list will be assigned to Table 1, the next four to Table 2, and three to other tables.

How to Start TGT

Start with the schedule of activities described in the following section. After teaching the lesson, announce team assignments and have students move their desks together to make team tables. Tell students that they will be working in teams for several weeks and competing in academic games to add points to their team scores, and that the highest-scoring teams will receive recognition in a class newsletter.

The first week of TGT is the hardest, but by the second week most students will settle into the pattern. Some students may complain about the teams to which they were assigned, but by the second week almost all such students find a way to get along with their teammates. Do not change team assignments after announcing them except under extreme circumstances, because it is students' realization that they will be in their team for several weeks that motivates them to work on getting along with their teammates instead of complaining about them.

Schedule of Activities

STAD consists of a regular cycle of instructional activities, as follows:

Teach—Present the lesson.

Team Study—Students work on worksheets in their teams to master the material.

Tournaments—Students play academic games in ability-homogeneous, three-member tournament tables.

Team Recognition—Team scores are computed based on team members' tournament scores, and a class newsletter or bulletin board recognizes high-scoring teams.

These activities are described in detail in the following pages.

TEACH

Time: One to two class periods
Main Idea: Present the lesson.
Materials Needed: Lesson plan

See the section on Teaching for STAD, p. 24.

TEAM STUDY

Time: One to two class periods
Main Idea: Students study worksheets in their teams.
Materials Needed:
  • Two *worksheets* for every *team*
  • Two *answer sheets* for every *team*

See the section on Team Study for STAD, pp. 24–25.

TOURNAMENTS

Time: One class period

Main Idea: Students compete at three-member, ability-homogeneous tournament
tables.

Materials Needed:

- Tournament Table Assignment Sheet, with tournament table assignments filled in
- One copy of Game Sheet and Game Answers (same as the quiz and quiz answers for STAD) for each tournament table
- One Game Score Sheet (copy from Appendix 5) for each tournament table
- One deck of number cards for each tournament table.

At the beginning of the tournament period, announce students' tournament table assignments and have them move desks together or go to tables serving as tournament tables. Have selected students help distribute one game sheet, one answer sheet, and one game score sheet to each table. Then begin the game. Figure 8 describes the game rules and procedures.

To start the game, the students draw cards to determine the first reader—the student drawing the highest number. Play proceeds in a clockwise direction from the first reader.

Game Rules (TGT)

Reader

1. Picks a numbered card and finds the corresponding question on the game sheet.
2. Reads the question out loud.
3. Tries to answer.

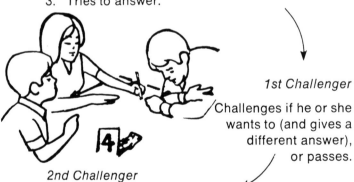

1st Challenger

Challenges if he or she wants to (and gives a different answer), or passes.

2nd Challenger

Challenges if 1st challenger passes, if he or she wants to. When all have challenged or passed, 2nd challenger checks the answer sheet. Whoever was *right* keeps the card. If the *reader* was wrong, there is no penalty, but if either challenger was wrong, he or she must put a previously won card, if any, back in the deck.

Figure 8

When the game begins, the reader shuffles the cards and picks the top one. He or she then reads aloud the question corresponding to the number on the card, including the possible answers if the question is multiple choice. For example, a student who picks card number 21 answers question number 21. A reader who is not sure of the answer is allowed to guess without penalty. If the content of the game involves math problems, all students (not just the reader) should work the problems so that they will be ready to challenge. After the reader gives an answer, the student to his or her left (first challenger) has the option of challenging and giving a different answer. If he or she passes, or if the second challenger has an answer different from that of the first two, the second challenger may challenge. Challengers have to be careful, however, because they lose a card (if they have one) if they are wrong. When everyone has answered, challenged, or passed, the second challenger checks the answer sheet and reads the right answer aloud. The player who gave the right answer keeps the card. If either challenger gave a wrong answer, he or she must return a previously won card (if any) to the deck. If no one gave a right answer, the card returns to the deck.

For the next round, everything moves one position to the left—the first challenger becomes the reader, the second challenger becomes the first challenger, and the reader becomes the second challenger. Play continues until the period ends or the deck is exhausted. When the game is over, players record the number of cards they won on the Game Score Sheet in the column marked "Game 1." If there is time, students reshuffle the deck and play a second game until the end of the period, recording the number of cards won under "Game 2" on the score sheet. (See Figure 9.)

All students should play the game at the same time. While they are playing, the teacher should move from group to group to answer questions and be sure that everyone understands the game procedures. Ten minutes before the end of the period, time should be called and students stop and count their cards. They should then fill in their names, teams, and scores on the Game Score Sheet, as in Figure 9.

Have students add up the scores they earned in each game (if they played more than one) and fill in their day's total. For younger children (fourth grade or below), simply collect the score sheets. If students are older, have them calculate their tournament points. Figure 10 summarizes tournament points for all possible outcomes. In general, have students give the top scorer six points, the second scorer four points, and the third scorer two points at a three-person table with no ties. If there are more or less than three players or if there any ties, use Figure 10 to tell students what to do. When everyone has calculated his or her tournament points, have a student collect the Game Score Sheets.

Bumping: Reassigning Students to Tournament Tables

Bumping, or reassigning students to new tournament tables, must be done after each tournament to prepare for the next tournament. It is easiest to do the bumping when figuring team scores and writing the newsletter.

To "bump" students, use the steps that follow. Figure 11 shows a diagram of the bumping procedures, and Figure 12 gives an example of a completed Tournament Table Assignment Sheet, showing how the bumping procedure works for a hypothetical class after two tournaments (one tournament per week).

1. Use the Game Score Sheets to identify the high and low scorers at each tournament table. On the Tournament Table Assignment Sheet, circle the table

Sample Game Score Sheet (TGT)

Player	Team	Game 1	Game 2	Game 3	Day's Total	Tournament Points
TABLE # ____	GAME SCORE SHEET (TGT)				ROUND # ____	
ERIC	GIANTS	5	7		12	2
LISA A.	GENIUSES	14	10		24	6
DARRYL	B. BOMBS	11	12		23	4

Figure 9

Calculating Tournament Points (TGT)

FOR A FOUR-PLAYER GAME

Player	No Ties	Tie For Top	Tie For Middle	Tie For Low	3-Way Tie For Top	3-Way Tie For Low	4-Way Tie	Tie For Low and High
Top Scorer	6 points	5	6	6	5	6	4	5
High Middle Scorer	4 points	5	4	4	5	3	4	5
Low Middle Scorer	3 points	3	4	3	5	3	4	3
Low Scorer	2 points	2	2	3	2	3	4	3

FOR A THREE-PLAYER GAME

Player	No Ties	Tie For Top Score	Tie For Low Score	3-Way Tie
Top Scorer	6 points	5	6	4
Middle Scorer	4 points	5	3	4
Low Scorer	2 points	2	3	4

FOR A TWO-PLAYER GAME

Player	No Ties	Tied
Top Scorer	6 points	4
Low Scorer	2 points	4

Figure 10

Bumping in TGT

T = Top Scorer   M = Middle Scorer   L = Low Scorer

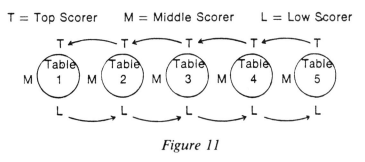

Figure 11

assignments of all students who were high scorers at their tables. If there was a tie for high score at any table, flip a coin to decide which number to circle; do not circle more than one number per table. In Figure 12, Tyrone, Maria, Tom, Carla, and Ralph were table winners in the first tournament, so their table numbers are circled in the first column; Tyrone, Liz, John T., Tanya, and Ruth were winners in the second tournament, so their numbers are circled in the second column.

2. Underline the table numbers of students who were low scorers. Again, if there was a tie for low score at any table, flip a coin to decide which to underline; do not underline more than one number per table. In Figure 12, Sarah, John T., John F., Kim, and Shirley were low scorers at their respective tables in the first tournament; Sam, Sylvia, Tom, John F., and Kim were low scorers in the second tournament.

3. Leave all other table assignments as they were, including numbers for absent students.

4. In the column for the next tournament, transfer the numbers as follows:
If the number is *circled*, reduce it by one (④ becomes 3). This means that the winner at Table 4 will compete at Table 3 the next week, a table where the competition will be more difficult. The only exception is that ① remains 1, because Table 1 is the highest table. If the number is *underlined*, increase it by one (4̲ becomes 5), except at the lowest table, where the low scorer stays at the same table (e.g., 1̲0̲ remains 10). This means that the low scorer at each table will compete the next week at a table where the competition will be less difficult. If the number is neither underlined nor circled, do not change it for the next tournament—transfer the same number.

In Figure 12, note that Tom won at Table 3 in the first tournament and was bumped up to Table 2. At Table 2 he was the low scorer, so for the third week's tournament he will compete at Table 3 again. Sylvia was the middle scorer at Table 3 in the first tournament, so she stayed at Table 3; then she lost in the second tournament and was moved to Table 4.

5. Count the number of students assigned to each table for the next week's tournament. Most tables should have three students; as many as two may have four. If table assignments do not work out this way, make some changes so that they do.

Note that in Figure 12, Tyrone won twice at Table 1, but did not change tables because there was no higher place to go than Table 1. Shirley and Kim lost at Table 5, but were not "bumped down" because Table 5 was the lowest table.

Sample Tournament Table Assignment Sheet with Bumping (TGT)

(Five Tournament Tables)
TOURNAMENT TABLE ASSIGNMENT SHEET (TGT)
Tournament Number:

Student	Team	1	2	3	4	5	6	7	8	9	10	11	12	13
SAM	Orioles	1	_1_	2										
SARAH	Cougars	_1_	2	2										
TYRONE	Whiz Kids	①	①	1										
MARIA	Geniuses	②	1	1										
LIZ	Orioles	2	②	1										
JOHN T.	Cougars	2	③	2										
SYLVIA	Whiz Kids	3	_3_	4										
TOM	Geniuses	③	2	3										
JOHN F.	Orioles	_3_	_4_	5										
TANYA	Whiz Kids	4	④	3										
CARLA	Orioles	④	3	3										
KIM	Cougars	4	5	5										
CARLOS	Geniuses	4	4	4										
SHIRLEY	Whiz Kids	5	5	5										
RALPH	Cougars	⑤	4	4										
RUTH	Geniuses	5	⑤	4										

Note:
③ indicates *high* scorer at Table 3
3 indicates *middle* scorer at Table 3
<u>3</u> indicates *low* scorer at Table 3

Results of ↑   ↑ Tournament Table
Most Recent   Assignment for
Tournament   Next Tournament

Figure 12

TEAM RECOGNITION

Main Idea: Figure team scores and prepare a class newsletter or bulletin board.

Figuring Team Scores

As soon as possible after the tournament, figure team scores and write the class newsletter to announce the standings. To do this, first check the tournament points on the Game Score Sheets. Then, simply transfer each student's tournament points to the Team Summary Sheet for his or her team, and add all the team members' scores. If the team has four members, the scoring is finished. However, if the team has more or fewer members than four, it will be necessary to transform the scores in order to compare team scores fairly. Appendix 1 gives transformed scores for all possible team sizes and number of points. For example, a five-member team with a total of 22 will receive a transformed score of 18. Consider only the transformed scores for three- or five-member teams in determining the team rank. Also record the cumulative team score to date on the Team Summary Sheet. Use the transformed score, of course, to figure the cumulative score.

Figure 13 shows the recording and totaling of scores for one team. Note that because this team has five members, the total team scores have been transformed to be comparable with those of four-member teams.

Sample Team Summary Sheet (TGT)

Team Name __GENIUSES__

Team Members	1	2	3	4	5	6	7	8	9	10
MARK	6	2	2	4						
KEVIN	4	4	2	6						
LISA A.	5	2	4	6						
JOHN F.	6	6	2	4						
DEWANDA	4	4	6	2						
Total Team Score	25	18	16	22						
Transformed Team Score	20	14	13	18						
Team Standing This Week	1	3	5	3						
Cumulative Score	20	34	47	65						
Cumulative Standing	1	1	2	2						

Figure 13

Recognizing Team Accomplishments

The motivational force that TGT generates is greatly enhanced by the use of public announcements, bulletin board displays, and newsletters to publicize the tournament results and indicate their importance. Of the three, the newsletter is perhaps the most effective method of creating a sense of excitement about the tournament and the students' performance.

The newsletter is also easy to produce. It can be written or typed on a ditto master and then run off and distributed to each student. It is important to distribute the newsletter as soon as possible after each tournament.

Once the Team Summary Sheets are completed (see Figure 13), it is easy to transfer the information for the last recorded tournament into the newsletter format. The Team Summary Sheets contain columns for several tournaments. After the sheets are completed, it is simply a matter of sorting them, once to rank the team scores for the latest tournament from highest to lowest, and once to rank the cumulative team scores. Thransfer the information to the newsletter.

Figure 14 depicts a sample TGT newsletter. Note that while this newsletter emphasizes team success, it also recognizes table winners, along with their teams. Rewards for winning teams such as refreshments, free time, or special privileges may be added to the newsletter recognition to make team success more important to students. See p. 27 for a discussion of such additional rewards.

Changing Teams

After five or six weeks of TGT, assign students to new teams.

Combining TGT with Other Activities

Teachers may wish to use TGT for part of their instruction, and other methods for other parts. For example, a science teacher might use TGT three days a week to teach basic science concepts, but then use related laboratory exercises on the other two days. TGT can also be used in combination with STAD, either by alternating quizzes one week and tournaments the next, or by having a quiz on the day after each tournament and counting both the quiz score and the tournament score toward the team score. This procedure gives the teacher a better idea of student progress than the tournament alone.

Grading

TGT does not automatically produce scores that can be used to compute individual grades. If this is a serious problem, consider using STAD instead of TGT. To determine individual grades, many teachers using TGT give a midterm and a final test each semester; some give a quiz after each tournament. Students' grades should be based on quiz scores or other individual assessments, not on tournament points or team scores. However, students' tournament points and/or team scores can be made a small part of their grades; or, if the school gives separate grades for effort, these scores can be used to determine the effort grades.

The Weekly Planet

4th Week March 28

LASH! Fantastic Four Sweeps Language Arts Tournament!

The Fantastic Four was the winning team this week with a total of 22 points. John T., ris, and Alvin put in outstanding performances for the Four, each contributing six points o their team. Their victory brings the Four to second place in the National League standings, only six points behind the leading Giants!

Hot on the heels of the Fantastic Four were the Brain Busters with 21 points. Anita nd Tanya helped the team out with victories at their tables, while Peter tied for first at is. The Brain Busters are still in third place in National League competition, but are oving up fast!

Third this week were the American League Geniuses with 18 points. They were helped out y Kevin and Lisa A., both table winners. Other table winners were Lisa P. of the Daredevils nd Mike of the Grammar Haters.

THIS WEEK'S SCORES

ST--Fantastic Four		2ND--Brain Busters		3RD--Geniuses	
John T.	6	Anita	6	Mark	4
Mary	4	Peter	5	Kevin	6
Kris	6	Darryl	4	Lisa A.	6
Alvin	6	Tanya	6	John F.	4
	22		21	Dewanda	2
					22/18

aredevils		Giants		Chipmunks		Grammar Haters	
isa P.	6	Robert	4	Caroline	5	Sarah	2
Henry	2	Eric	2	Jerry	2	Willy	2
indi	4	Sharon	2	Charlene	3	Mike	6
red	4	Sylvia	4	James	2	Theresa	3
						John H.	2
	16		12		12		15/12

SEASON'S STANDING FOURTH WEEK

National League		American League	
AM	SEASON SCORE	TEAM	SEASON SCORE
ants	78	Grammar Haters	74
ntastic Four	72	Geniuses	65
ain Busters	66	Daredevils	57
ipmunks	59		

Figure 14

JIGSAW II

Overview

Jigsaw II can be used whenever the material to be studied is in written narrative form. It is most appropriate in such subjects as social studies, literature, some parts of science, and related areas in which concepts rather than skills are the learning goals. The instructional "raw material" for Jigsaw II should usually be a chapter, a story, a biography, or similar narrative or descriptive material.

In Jigsaw II, students work in heterogeneous teams as in STAD and TGT. Students are assigned chapters or other units to read, and are given "Expert Sheets" that contain different topics for each team member to focus on when reading. When everyone has finished reading, students from different teams with the same topic meet in an "expert group" to discuss their topic for about 30 minutes. The experts then return to their teams and take turns teaching their teammates about their topics. Finally, students take quizzes that cover all the topics, and the quiz scores become team scores as in STAD. Also as in STAD, the scores that students contribute to their teams are based on the individual improvement score system, and high-scoring teams and individuals are recognized in a newsletter or bulletin board. Thus, students are motivated to study the material well and to work hard in their expert groups so that they can help their team do well. The key to Jigsaw is interdependence—every student depends on teammates to provide the information he or she needs to do well on the quizzes.

Preparing to Use Jigsaw II

Materials

Before beginning, make an Expert Sheet and a quiz for each unit of material. At present, Johns Hopkins Team Learning Project materials are available for Jigsaw only in junior high school U.S. History, but preparing these materials is not difficult. Appendix 4 presents an example of a complete Jigsaw II unit.

To make materials for Jigsaw II follow these steps:

1. Select several chapters, stories, or other units, each covering material for a two- to three-day unit. If students are to read in class, the selections should not require more than a half hour to complete; if the reading is to be assigned for homework, the selections can be longer.

2. Make an Expert Sheet for each unit. This tells students what to concentrate on while they read, and which expert group they will work with. It identifies four topics that are central to the unit. For example, an Expert Sheet for a level four social studies book might refer to a section on the Blackfoot Indian tribes that is used to illustrate a number of concepts about groups, group norms, leadership, and so on. The Expert Sheet for that section might be as follows:

Expert Sheet
"The Blackfoot"

To read: Pages 3–9 and 11–12.

Topics:
1. How were Blackfoot men expected to act?
2. What is a group and what does it do?
   What are the most important groups for the Blackfoot?
3. What did Blackfoot bands and clubs do?
4. What were the Blackfoot customs and traditions?

As much as possible, the topics should cover themes that appear throughout the chapter, instead of issues that appear only once. For example, if the class were reading *Tom Sawyer*, a good topic might be "How did Tom feel about his community?" which appears throughout the book, as opposed to "What happened to Tom and Huck Finn when they ran away?" which a student could learn by reading only a section of the book. Also see the example of topics based on the Introduction to this publication that appears in Appendix 4. The expert topics may be put on ditto masters and one copy run off for each student, or they may be put on the chalkboard or poster paper.

3. Make a quiz for each unit. The quiz should consist of at least eight questions, two for each topic, or some multiple of four (e.g., 12, 16, 20), to make an equal number of questions for each topic. Teachers may wish to add two or more general questions to give the quiz an even number of items. The questions should require considerable understanding, because students will have had ample time to discuss their topics in depth, and easy questions would fail to challenge those who have done a good job in preparation. However, the questions should not be obscure. In the Blackfoot example, the first two questions might be as follows:

1A: Which of the following was *not* an expected way of behaving for a Blackfoot man?
   a. He was expected to be brave.
   b. He was expected to brag about how many of the enemy tribe he had touched.
   c. He was expected to clean buffalo meat.
   d. He was expected to share buffalo meat.
1B: What are norms of behavior?
   a. All the ways of acting that people in a group have
   b. The ways people in a group expect themselves and other members of the group to act
   c. Records of great deeds
   d. Sharing food with the very old

All students must answer all questions. The quiz should take no more than ten minutes. Teachers may wish to use an activity other than a quiz or in addition to a quiz as an opportunity for team members to show their learning—for example, an oral report, a written report, a crafts project. A sample Jigsaw II quiz appears in Appendix 4.

4. Use discussion outlines (optional). A discussion outline for each topic can help guide the discussions in the expert groups. It should list the points that students should definitely consider in discussing their topics. For example, a discussion outline for a topic relating to the settlement of the English colonies in America is as follows:

Topic: What role did religious ideals play in the establishment of settlement in America?

Discussion Outline

—Puritan beliefs and religious practices
—Puritan treatment of dissenters
—Founding of Connecticut and Rhode Island
—Quakers and the establishment of Pennsylvania
—Catholics and religious toleration in Maryland

Assigning Students to Teams

Assign students to four- or five-member heterogeneous teams exactly as in STAD (see pp. 21–23). Place team members' names on Team Summary Sheets, leaving the team name blank.

Determining Initial Base Scores

Rank students on past performance and assign them initial base scores exactly as for STAD (see p. 23). Use a Quiz Score Sheet to record the initial base scores (see Appendix 5).

How to Start Jigsaw II

Start with the schedule of activities described in the following section. Announce team assignments and tell students that they will be working in teams for several weeks. Tell them they will study different topics and teach their teams what they have learned, the teams will be quizzed on all topics, and the highest-scoring teams will be recognized in a class newsletter. Pass the Expert Sheet and assign students to topics; then have students read the material. When they have finished, have all students with the same topics meet in Expert Groups to discuss them. (If any Expert Group has more than six students, split it into two groups.) After the discussion, have students return to their teams to teach their teammates what they have learned. Then give all students the quiz. The first week of Jigsaw II is the hardest, but by the second week most students will settle into the pattern.

Schedule of Activities

Jigsaw II consists of a regular cycle of instructional activities as follows:

Text—Students receive expert topics and read assigned material to locate information.

Talk—Students with the same expert topics meet to discuss them in expert groups.

Team Report—Experts return to their teams to teach their topics to their teammates.

Test—Students take individual quizzes covering all topics.

Team Recognition—Team scores are computed as in STAD.

These activities are described in detail in the following pages.

TEXT

Time: One-half to one class period (or assign for homework)

Main Idea: Students receive expert topics and read assigned material to locate information on their topics.

Materials Needed:
- An Expert Sheet for each student, consisting of four expert topics.
- A text or other reading assignment on which the expert topics for each student are based.

The first activity in Jigsaw II is distribution of texts and expert topics, assignment of topics to individual students, and reading. Pass out Expert Sheets; then randomly assign students to take each topic (go to each team and point out students for each one). If any team has five members, have two students take Topic 1 together.

When students have their topics, let them read their materials. Or the reading may be assigned as homework. Students who finish reading before others can go back and make notes.

TALK

Time: One-half class period

Main Idea: Students with the same expert topics discuss them in expert groups.

Materials Needed:
- Expert Sheet and texts for each student
- (Optional) Discussion outlines for each topic; one for each student with that topic.

Have all students with Expert Topic 1 get together at one table, all students with Expert Topic 2 at another, and so on. If any expert group has more than 7 students (that is, if the class has more than 28 students), split the expert group into two smaller groups.

If students are to use a discussion outline, distribute it to each expert group.

Appoint a *discussion leader* for each group. The discussion leader need not be a particularly able student, and all students should have an opportunity to play that role at some time. The leader's job is to moderate the discussion, calling on group members who raise their hands, and trying to see that everyone participates.

Give the expert groups about 20 minutes to discuss their topics. Students should try to locate information on their topics in their texts and share the information with the group. Group members should take notes on all points discussed.

While the expert groups are working, the teacher should circulate through the class, spending time with each group in turn. Teachers may wish to answer questions and resolve misunderstandings, but they should not try to take over leadership of the groups—that is the discussion leaders' responsibility. They may need to remind discussion leaders that part of their job is to see that everyone participates.

TEAM REPORT

Time: One-half class period

Main Idea: "Experts" return to their teams to teach their topics to their teammates.

Experts should return to their teams to teach their topics to their teammates. They should take about five minutes to review everything they have learned about their topics from their reading and their discussions in the expert groups.

If two students on any team shared Topic 1, they should make a joint presentation.

Emphasize that students have a responsibility to their teammates to be good teachers as well as good listeners.

Teachers may hold a brief whole-class discussion after team reports are completed.

TEST

Time: One-half class period

Main Idea: Students take quiz.

Materials Needed:

• One copy of the quiz for each student.

Distribute the quizzes and give students adequate time for almost everyone to finish. Have students exchange quizzes with members of other teams for scoring, or collect the quizzes for teacher scoring. If students do the scoring, have the checkers put their names at the bottom of the quizzes they checked. After class, spot check several quizzes to be sure that students did a good job of checking.

TEAM RECOGNITION

Scoring for Jigsaw II is the same as that for STAD, including base scores, improvement points, and team scoring procedures. Also as in STAD, newsletters, bulletin boards, and/or other rewards recognize high-scoring teams (see p. 27). Since Jigsaw units rarely have 30 items, it is necessary to give more than one point per item to stay close to 30 points for the quiz. (Approximately 30 points are needed to figure improvement scores.) Give the following number of points per item to make Jigsaw II quizzes approach 30 points:

Number of Quiz Items	Points per Item
8	4
12	2½
16	2
20	1½

ORIGINAL JIGSAW

Aronson's original Jigsaw resembles Jigsaw II in most respects, but it also has some important differences. In the original Jigsaw, students read individual sections entirely different from those read by their teammates. This has the benefit of making the experts possessors of completely unique information, and thus makes the teams value each member's contribution more highly. For example, in a unit on Chile, one student might have information on Chile's economy, another on its geography, a third on its history, etc. To know all about Chile, students must rely on their teammates. Original Jigsaw also takes less time than Jigsaw II; its readings are shorter, only a part of the total unit to be studied.

The most difficult part of original Jigsaw, and the reason that Jigsaw II is presented first in this publication, is that each individual section must be written so that it is comprehensible by itself. Existing materials cannot be used as in Jigsaw II; books can rarely be divided neatly into sections that make any sense without the other sections. For example, in a biography of Alexander Hamilton, the section describing his duel with Aaron Burr would assume that the reader knew who both men were (having read the rest of the biography). Preparing an original Jigsaw unit involves rewriting material to fit the Jigsaw format. The added advantage of Jigsaw II is that all students read all the material, which may make unified concepts easier to understand.

Teachers who wish to use original Jigsaw to capitalize on its special features giving the experts unique information (which may contribute to Jigsaw's positive effects on student self-esteem) can use Jigsaw II with these modifications:

1. Write units that present unique information abut a subject but make sense by themselves. This can be done by cutting apart texts and adding information as needed, or by writing completely new material.

2. Assign students to five- or six-member teams and make five topics for each unit.

3. Appoint team leaders, and emphasize team-building exercises before and during use of the technique. Team-building involves activities that help the teams learn how to work well together and to get to know one another. Part of team-building after the beginning is process analysis—asking members to analyze the strengths and weaknesses of their team operation.

4. Use quizzes less frequently and do not use team scores, improvement scores, or newsletters. Simply give students individual grades.

For more information on original Jigsaw, see *The Jigsaw Classroom* (1).

Other Ways of Using Jigsaw

Jigsaw is one of the most flexible of the Student Team Learning methods. Several modifications can be made that keep the basic model but change the details of implementation.

1. Instead of having the topics refer to narrative materials given to students, have students search a set of classroom or library materials to find information on their topics.

2. Have students write essays or give oral reports instead of taking quizzes after completing the experts' reports.

3. Instead of having all teams study the same material, give each team a unique topic to learn together and each team member a subtopic. The team could then prepare and make an oral presentation to the entire class. This strategy is described in detail by Sharan and Sharan (16).

TEAM ACCELERATED INSTRUCTION (TAI)

Team Accelerated Instruction, or TAI, is not described completely in this book because it cannot be used in the classroom from a description alone (in contrast to STAD, TGT, and Jigsaw). Information on mathematics materials and teachers' manuals designed for TAI may be obtained from the Johns Hopkins Team Learning Project (see the Preface). However, an overview of TAI follows.

Overview

Application

TAI is designed for use in all grades 2–8 mathematics classes, except junior high algebra classes.

Teams

Students are assigned to four- to five-member, heterogeneous teams as in STAD, TGT, and Jigsaw II.

Placement Test

Students are pretested on mathematics operations and placed at the appropriate point in the individualized program based on their test performance.

Curriculum Materials

For all operations skills (addition, subtraction, multiplication, division, numeration, decimals, fractions, ratios, percent, algebra, and word problems), students work on individualized curriculum materials that have the following subparts:

1. A guide page explaining the skill to be mastered and giving a step-by-step method of solving problems.
2. Several skill pages, each consisting of 20 problems. Each skill page introduces a subskill that leads to final mastery of the entire skill. For example, a unit on adding with renaming consists of a skill page on decoding whether or not renaming is necessary, a second skill page on adding the tens column, and a final skill page on adding the ones column, performing the renaming, and adding the tens column to get the final answer.
3. A formative test consisting of two parallel sets of 10 items.
4. A unit test.
5. Answer sheets for skill pages, formative tests, and unit tests.

Students work on these individualized units for three in every four weeks. During each fourth week, skills other than operations, such as geometry, sets and measurement, are taught using group-paced methods. These units are not included in the individualized materials because they do not require the level of prior skills needed for the operations units; therefore they can be taught more efficiently to the entire class.

Team Study Method

After they take the diagnostic test, students are assigned a starting place in the individualized mathematics units. They work on their units in teams, exchanging answer sheets with partners. Students work four problems on their skill pages, and then check with their partners. If all four problems are correct, they may go on to the next skill page; if not, they must work the next four problems, until four in a row are correct. If students have difficulty with the sets of four problems, they may call on a teammate or the teacher for help. When students have finished all skill pages, they may take a ten-item formative test; if they answer eight or more items correctly, they may take the unit test. One of three student monitors selected each day scores the tests.

Team Scores

At the end of each week, the teacher compiles a team score. Teams receive ten points for every unit completed by any team member, plus two points for each perfect paper, and one point for each paper with only one incorrect answer.

Team Recognition

Criteria are established for team performance. Meeting a high criterion qualifies a team as a "Superteam," meeting a moderate criterion qualifies a team as a "Goodteam." Members of such teams receive certificates.

Teaching Groups

Every day the teacher works for 15 to 20 minutes with at least one group of six to ten students who are at about the same point in the curriculum. The purpose of these sessions is to go over concepts, explain any points causing students trouble, and prepare students for upcoming units. During this time, other students continue working on their own units.

Curriculum Organization

The curriculum is organized into 12 skills: addition, subtraction, multiplication, division, fractions, decimals, numeration, percent, ratios, statistics, algebra, and word problems. The units in each skill area are arranged in a definite sequence in which each unit depends on mastery of the last unit.

COOPERATIVE INTEGRATED READING AND COMPOSITION (CIRC)

The CIRC program consists of three principal elements: basal-related activities, direct instruction in reading comprehension, and integrated language arts/writing. In all these activities, students work in heterogeneous learning teams. All activities follow a regular cycle that involves teacher presentation, team practice, independent practice, peer pre-assessment, additional practice, and testing. As is the case for TAI, CIRC has its own manual and materials, and therefore cannot be implemented from this book alone. The major components of the CIRC program are described in the following pages.

Reading Groups

Students are assigned to two or three reading groups according to their reading level, as determined by their teachers.

Teams

Students are assigned to pairs (or triads) within their reading groups, and then the pairs are assigned to teams composed of partnerships from two reading groups. For example, a team might be composed of two students from the top reading group and two from the low group. Team members receive points based on their individual performances on all quizzes, compositions, and book reports, and these points are contributed to form a team score. Teams that meet an average criterion of 95 percent on all activities in a given week are designated "Superteams" and receive attractive certificates; those that meet an average criterion of 90 percent are designated "Greatteams" and receive smaller certificates.

Basal-Related Activities

Students use their regular basal readers. Basal stories are introduced and discussed in teacher-led reading groups that meet for approximately 20 minutes each day. During these groups, teachers set a purpose for reading, introduce new vocabulary, review old vocabulary, discuss the story after students have read it, and so on. Presentation methods for each segment of the lesson are structured. For example, teachers use a vocabulary presentation procedure that requires a demonstration of understanding of word meaning by each individual, a review of methods of word attack, and repetitive oral reading of vocabulary to achieve fluency. Story discussions are structured to emphasize such skills as making and supporting predictions and identifying the problem in a narrative.

After stories are introduced, students are given a story packet, which lays out a series of activities for them to do in their teams when they are not working with the teacher in a reading group. The sequence of activities is as follows:

- *Partner Reading.* Students read the story silently and then take turns reading it aloud with their partners, alternating on each paragraph. Meanwhile the listener corrects any errors the reader may make. The teacher assesses student performance by circulating and listening in as students read to each other.

- *Story Grammar and Story-Related Writing.* Students are given questions ("Treasure Hunts") related to each narrative emphasizing the grammar, the structure that underlies all narratives. Halfway through the story, they are instructed to stop reading and to identify the characters, the setting, and the problem in the story, and to predict how the problem will be resolved. At the end of the story students respond to the story as a whole and write a few paragraphs on a related topic (for example, they might be asked to write a different ending).

- *Words Out Loud.* Students are given a list of new or difficult words used in the story that they must be able to read correctly in any order without hesitating or stumbling. Students practice these word lists with their partners or other teammates until they can read them smoothly.

- *Word Meaning.* Students are given a list of story words that are new in their speaking vocabularies and are asked to look them up in a dictionary, paraphrase the definition, and write a sentence for each that shows the meaning of the word (i.e., "An *octopus* grabbed the swimmer with its eight long legs," not "I have an *octopus*.").

- *Story Retell.* After reading the story and discussing it in their reading groups, students summarize the main points to their partners.

- *Spelling.* Students pretest one another on a list of spelling words each week, and then work over the course of the week to help one another master the list. Students use a "disappearing list" strategy in which they make new lists of missed words after each assessment until the list disappears and they go back to the full list, repeating the process as many times as necessary.

- *Partner Checking.* After students complete each of the activities listed above, their partners initial a student assignment form indicating that they have completed and/or achieved criteria on that task. Students are given daily expectations as to the number of activities to be completed, but they can go at their own rate and complete the activities earlier if they wish, creating additional time for independent reading (see below).

- *Tests.* At the end of three class periods, students are given a comprehension test on the story, are asked to write meaningful sentences for each vocabulary word, and are asked to read the word list aloud to the teacher. Students are not permitted to help one another on these tests. The test scores and evaluations of the story-related writing are major components of students' weekly team scores.

Direct Instruction in Reading Comprehension

One day each week, students receive direct instruction in specific reading comprehension skills (e.g., identifying main ideas, understanding causal relations, making inferences). A special step-by-step curriculum was designed for this purpose. After each lesson, students work on reading comprehension worksheets and/or games as a whole team, first gaining consensus on one set of worksheet items and then assessing one another and discussing any remaining problems on a second set of items.

Integrated Language Arts and Writing

During language arts periods, teachers use a specific language arts/writing curriculum especially developed for CIRC. In it, students work as teams on language arts skills that lead directly to writing activities. The emphasis of this curriculum is on writing; language mechanics skills are introduced as specific aids to writing rather than as separate topics. For example, students study modifiers during a lesson on writing descriptive paragraphs, and they study quotation marks as a part of writing dialogue in the context of a narrative. The writing program uses both "writers' workshops" in which students write on topics of their choice, and specific, teacher-directed writing lessons focused on such skills as writing compare/contrast paragraphs, newspaper articles, mystery stories, and letters. On all writing assignments students draft compositions after consultation about their ideas and organizational plans with their teammates and the teacher; they work with teammates to revise the content of their compositions; then they edit one another's work using peer editing forms emphasizing grammatical and mechanical correctness. The peer editing forms begin very simply, but as students cover successive skills the forms are made increasingly complex. Finally, students "publish" their final compositions in team and/or class books.

Independent Reading

Every evening, students are asked to read a trade book of their choice for at least twenty minutes. Parents initial forms indicating that students have read the required time, and students contribute points to their teams if they submit a completed form each week. Students also complete at least one book report every two weeks, for which they also receive team points. Independent reading and book reports replace all other homework in reading and language arts. If students complete their story packets or other activities early, they may also read their independent reading books in class.

TROUBLESHOOTING

As they use student Team Learning, teachers may experience a few problems. Some of these problems and the solutions that other teachers have found effective are discussed in the following pages.

1. Team Members Not Getting Along. This problem often comes up in the first week or two of use of Student Team Learning. Remember, a team is made up of the most unlikely combination possible. Students differ from one another in sex, ethnicity, and academic performance level.

The primary solution for this problem is time. Some students will be unhappy about their team assignments initially, but as soon as they realize that they will be working in the teams for a long time, and especially when they receive their first team scores and realize that they really are a team and need to cooperate to be successful, they will find a way to get along. For this reason, it is important not to allow students to change teams; what makes the teammates work on their problems is the recognition that they will be together for many weeks.

Some students, however, will need constant reminding that their task is to cooperate with their teammates. It is important to set a firm tone that cooperation with teammates is appropriate behavior during team practice. No one should be forced to work with a team; individuals who refuse (this happens rarely) should be allowed to work alone until they are ready to join the team. However, it should be clear to students that putdowns, making fun of teammates, or refusing to help them are ineffective ways for teams to be successful and not acceptable kinds of behavior.

One effective way to improve student cooperation is to provide extra rewards to winning teams. Sometimes students will not care how the team or their teammates are doing until they know that the winning team will receive refreshments, time off, release from a test, and so on. Some teachers give the members of the week's winning team an automatic A grade for the week.

It is also a good idea to have students who work in pairs within their teams switch partners from time to time, to reemphasize the need for team effort, not just individual preparation.

If some teams do not work out, the teacher may decide to change teams after three or four weeks instead of six, reassigning students in ways that avoid the problems encountered in the first team assignments.

2. Misbehavior. One way to encourage students to behave appropriately is to give each team up to three additional team points each day based on the team's behavior, cooperativeness, and effort. In such cases, it is also important that the teacher move from team to team telling them what they are doing right (for example, "I see the Cougars working well together. . . . The Fantastic Four are all in their seats and doing their work. . . . The Chiefs are working quietly.") The points earned for team behavior should definitely not be a surprise, but should reflect teacher comments during the period.

3. Noise. Noise is more of a problem in some schools than others, depending on acoustics, open versus traditional construction, and school attitudes toward noise. Student Team Learning does not go well with the teacher shushing students every five minutes, but if things are so noisy that students cannot hear each other, something should be done.

The first solution to try for the noise problem is to bring all activity to a stop, get absolute quiet, and then whisper a reminder to students to speak softly. Students should be taught to stop talking immediately when the lights are flicked off for a moment, or a bell sounds, or some other signal is given. If this does not work, try to make noise level part of the criteria for earning extra team points just noted.

If students can hear each other and not get out of hand, try to learn to tolerate their on-task noise if possible.

4. Absences. Student absenteeism can be a major problem in a Student Team Learning class because students depend on one another to contribute points to the team. The solution, however, is relatively simple in classrooms where absenteeism is not extremely high. When students miss a tournament or a quiz, prorate the scores for their teams that week, using Appendix 1. For example, if one student on a four-member team was absent for the tournament or quiz, prorate that team's score as for a three-member team.

When Student Team Learning is to be used in a class with very poor attendance, poor attenders should be distributed evenly among teams as fifth or sixth members, so that at least three or four students will be likely to show up on each team each day. If there are some students who never or almost never attend, they may be left out of the team system and reincluded if they start coming to class more regularly.

5. Ineffective Use of Team Practice Time. If students do not use their time in team practice effectively, the teacher can impose some kind of structure on the team practice sessions to be sure that they use the time well.

One problem is that students may be used to doing their worksheets alone and thinking they are finished when they reach the end, whether or not they or their teammates understand the material. This problem is dealt with primarily by providing only two worksheets per team so that students have to work together. Teachers can also make (or have students make) flashcards with questions on one side and answers on the other, and have students drill each other in pairs or threes, putting correctly answered items in one pile and missed items in another. Students go through the missed pile until they have correctly answered everything once, and then go through the entire set again until each student can achieve 100% on the items in any order. This will work only if the answers are short. If the answers require figuring, as in most of mathematics, then students should work in pairs or threes, going through the items one at a time and checking answers after everyone has finished each item. If anyone missed a question, any teammates who answered it correctly should explain what they did. In either of these cases, students should change partners within their teams every 30 minutes or so, to make sure that teammates do not form little subteams.

53

6. Performance Level Range Too Wide for Group Instruction. If teachers have this problem, it is first important to think about what they were doing before using Student Team Learning. Those who were using whole-group instruction can use Student Team Learning, but they need to take time to work with low performers to help get them up to the level of the rest of the class. Teachers of grades two to eight should use TAI or CIRC if they can obtain these materials; since these programs accommodate instruction to individual needs, they can solve the problem of a wide performance range.

7. Problems with the TGT Tournament. Usually there are few tournament problems that cannot be handled by simply making a rules interpretation. The problems that arise often come from a misreading of the rules or of the manual. For example, some teachers do not allow students to reshuffle the cards at the end of one game and go through the deck again. Many teachers complain that students at the higher tables do not want to play the game again, so they provide extra resource material for those students to work with. Nevertheless, if at all possible, encourage students to play two or more games if they finish theirs first. Make sure, however, that while game scores are recorded after each game, tournament points are computed only once, at the end of the period; the maximum tournament points a player may earn is always six, no matter how many games are played. Although students should be allowed to play the game more than once, the teacher should call time when it is obvious that the entire class has gone through the cards at least once and is not eager to continue.

Another frequent misreading of the TGT game rules involves challenges. If a student challenges and is wrong, he or she returns a previously won card (if any) to the deck. Students never give each other cards they have won previously.

At times players complain that certain students had more chances than others to earn points because of their starting positions. This is a serious problem when some tables are getting 90 to 100 percent of the items correct, and one extra turn may determine the winner. To create a totally fair competition, first be sure that the number of items is a multiple of the number of players (for example, 30 items for three players). For four-person tournament tables, simply remove two number cards from the deck to get the correct multiple (for example, 28 items for four players). Thus, for any table where all items are answered correctly, players will have an equal chance to win. When you call time to end the tournament, let any tables where all players have not had an equal number of turns continue to play until everyone has had the same number of turns.

Occasionally a teacher will have some students who just cannot handle the competition. If this is a widespread problem, switch to STAD. If it is a problem for only a few students, withdraw a student from the competition, give him or her the game sheet as a quiz, and grade the quiz on a scale of two to six to correspond to a TGT score.

8. Problems with STAD. Almost all problems with STAD are problems with teams, discussed earlier. However, STAD has one additional problem. Because of the use of the individual improvement score system, some previously high-performing students (and occasionally their parents) complain that it is not fair that they have to do so much better to get the same points as a low-performing student. To answer this concern, emphasize the following:

a. The individual improvement score system is fair because in order to earn maximum points, everyone has to show improvement each week, not just

54

perform at the same level as before. Improving by ten points is just as hard for a low-performing student as it is for a high-performing student.

    b. Because a maximum of ten points is possible, and because a perfect paper is always worth ten points, no student with a low base score can earn a higher number of points than one with the best possible quiz score.

    c. Although team points are based on improvement, grades are still determined in the usual way. Thus, high-performing students who continue to perform at a high level will still receive high grades.

Another problem that arises with STAD is that occasionally, because a particular quiz is very difficult, almost everyone will get zero points. When this happens, give each item 1½ or 2 points, because it is unfair to penalize the entire class if the test is too difficult. If large numbers of students keep performing below their base scores, the material being taught is probably above the level of the class, and either the pace should be slowed or more appropriate material chosen.

9. Problems with Jigsaw. Team presentations in Jigsaw are so structured that little can go wrong with them, except that students should be held to a firm time limit for each presentation in order not to take up too much class time.

The expert groups are much less concretely structured and thus more prone to problems. When students do not seem to be using their expert group time well, the general solution is to provide more structure.

Some teachers provide a set of discussion topics for expert groups and have the expert group leader call on students to contribute to each discussion. Another way to make the expert groups more effective is to have an aide, parent, or older student act as discussion leader. Also, the teacher may be able to stagger the schedule of expert groups so that she or he can work with each group. Most expert groups do not need this kind of help, but when students are either young or lack self-organization skills, they need some additional structure.

Absenteeism is a special problem in Jigsaw because it is important for every team to have an expert on every topic. One way to deal with very serious absenteeism is to make six-member teams and have students work on each of three topics in pairs, so that at least one student is likely to appear for each topic. Another solution is to make the readings very short, so that students can read, discuss their topics in their expert groups, and take their quizzes all in the same period. Or reduce the number of topics to three—at least three students are likely to be present to take the topics, and this averts the problem of absent team members.

10. Scoring Problems. Teachers often find several things about scoring difficult or confusing.

Bumping in TGT is not usually a serious problem, except that teachers need to be prepared to reassign students when someone assigned to a particular tournament table is absent. Also, new students should not automatically be assigned to the bottom of the bumping scheme. This gives them a considerable advantage until they are bumped "up" to the proper table. New students should be assigned to tables on the basis of some test or past grade.

Team scores also present few problems. Some teachers forget to prorate for teams larger or smaller than four members. This gives teams an unfair advantage or disadvantage; prorating is very important.

The individual improvement score system used in STAD and Jigsaw II is not very difficult either, but mistakes are sometimes made. It is essential to remember that the maximum improvement score is ten and that perfect quizzes get ten points regardless of the base score. It is also essential to readjust base scores every two weeks. Not doing so is a serious problem, because a student whose base score was set too low or too high and is not changed has an unfair advantage or disadvantage. Some teachers give students zeros for skipping class or for some disciplinary problem. Give students zero improvement points toward their team score if they skip class, but never count these scores as zeros in refiguring base scores; consider them blank for that purpose.

11. Too Much Work for Teachers. "Too much work" is the most frequently heard complaint about Student Team Learning from teachers, especially from those who are making their own materials. However, there are some ways to reduce the work required.

One way is to have students help with the scoring and newsletter writing. Responsibility for writing the newsletter can be passed from team to team, and volunteer students can come in after school to help score quizzes, calculate team scores, or do the bumping for TGT. Scoring quizzes is the biggest job in terms of teacher time, but it is also the easiest to get help with; students can either exchange papers in class or entire classes can exchange papers. Volunteer students can also make ditto masters and run off materials.

For teachers using the Johns Hopkins Team Learning Project materials, additional curriculum material is not difficult to make. However, it is a bigger job for those who are making materials from scratch. In such cases, the best arrangement is for teachers in the same department or grade level to cooperate in making a set of materials, with each teacher taking responsibility for part of the curriculum. The result will be a central library of curriculum materials that all teachers can use. Existing worksheets and quizzes from previous years can also be incorporated into this library, and whenever teachers add a unit, it, too, can be made available for colleagues to use.

OTHER COOPERATIVE LEARNING METHODS

Although the majority of teachers who use Student Team Learning in their classrooms use STAD, TGT, Jigsaw, TAI, CIRC, or some combination of these methods, many have seen the need to modify the basic techniques for particular purposes or special situations. Several extensions or modifications of Student Team Learning have been created to meet special needs. These modifications are described in *Using Student Team Learning* (22), which can be obtained from the Johns Hopkins Team Learning Project (see the Preface).

Appendixes

APPENDIX 1
Prorating Scores for Teams with Two, Three, or Five Members

Raw Scores	Five-Member Team	Three-Member Team	Two-Member Team
4			8
5			10
6		8	12
7		9	14
8		11	16
9		12	18
10	8	13	20
11	9	15	22
12	10	16	24
13	11	17	26
14	12	19	28
15	12	20	30
16	13	21	32
17	14	23	34
18	14	24	36
19	15	25	38
20	16	27	40
21	17	28	
22	18	29	
23	18	31	
24	19	32	
25	20	33	
26	21	35	
27	22	36	
28	22	37	
29	23	39	
30	24	40	
31	25		
32	26		
33	26		
34	27		
35	28		
36	29		
37	30		
38	30		
39	31		
40	32		
41	33		
42	35		
43	34		
44	35		
45	36		
46	37		
47	38		
48	38		
49	39		
50	40		

APPENDIX 2
Calculating New Base Scores

To find the new base score, add the student's two quiz scores together, and find the total in the column to the left. Fin the student's old base score at the top. Follow the row across and the column down until you come to where the intersect. This number is the student's new base score.

Total of Quiz Scores	Old Base Score										
	3	4	5	6	7	8	9	10	11	12	13
16	3	3	4	4	4	5	5	5	6	6	6
17	3	4	4	4	5	5	5	6	6	6	7
18	4	4	4	5	5	5	6	6	6	7	7
19	4	4	5	5	5	6	6	6	7	7	7
20	4	5	5	5	6	6	6	7	7	7	8
21	5	5	5	6	6	6	7	7	7	8	8
22	5	5	6	6	6	7	7	7	8	8	8
23	5	6	6	6	7	7	7	8	8	8	9
24	6	6	6	7	7	7	8	8	8	9	9
25	6	6	7	7	7	8	8	8	9	9	9
26	6	7	7	7	8	8	8	9	9	9	10
27	7	7	7	8	8	8	9	9	9	10	10
28	7	7	8	8	8	9	9	9	10	10	10
29	7	8	8	8	9	9	9	10	10	10	11
30	8	8	8	9	9	9	10	10	10	11	11
31	8	8	9	9	9	10	10	10	11	11	11
32	8	9	9	9	10	10	10	11	11	11	12
33	9	9	9	10	10	10	11	11	11	12	12
34	9	9	10	10	10	11	11	11	12	12	12
35	9	10	10	10	11	11	11	12	12	12	13
36	10	10	10	11	11	11	12	12	12	13	13
37	10	10	11	11	11	12	12	12	13	13	13
38	10	11	11	11	12	12	12	13	13	13	14
39	11	11	11	12	12	12	13	13	13	14	14
40	11	11	12	12	12	13	13	13	14	14	14
41	11	12	12	12	13	13	13	14	14	14	15
42	12	12	12	13	13	13	14	14	14	15	15
43	12	12	13	13	13	14	14	14	15	15	15
44	12	13	13	13	14	14	14	15	15	15	16
45	13	13	13	14	14	14	15	15	15	16	16
46	13	13	14	14	14	15	15	15	16	16	16
47	13	14	14	14	15	15	15	16	16	16	17
48	14	14	14	15	15	15	16	16	16	17	17
49	14	14	15	15	15	16	16	16	17	17	17
50	14	15	15	15	16	16	16	17	17	17	18
51	15	15	15	16	16	16	17	17	17	18	18
52	15	15	16	16	16	17	17	17	18	18	18
53	15	16	16	16	17	17	17	18	18	18	19
54	16	16	16	17	17	17	18	18	18	19	19
55	16	16	17	17	17	18	18	18	19	19	19
56	16	17	17	17	18	18	18	19	19	19	20
57	17	17	17	18	18	18	19	19	19	20	20
58	17	17	18	18	18	19	19	19	20	20	20
59	17	18	18	18	19	19	19	20	20	20	21
60	18	18	18	19	19	19	20	20	20	21	21

Old Base Score

Total of Quiz Scores	14	15	16	17	18	19	20	21	22	23	24	25
16	7	7	7	8	8	8	9	9	9	10	10	10
17	7	7	8	8	8	9	9	9	10	10	10	11
18	7	8	8	8	9	9	9	10	10	10	11	11
19	8	8	8	9	9	9	10	10	10	11	11	11
20	8	8	9	9	9	10	10	10	11	11	11	12
21	8	9	9	9	10	10	10	11	11	11	12	12
22	9	9	9	10	10	10	11	11	11	12	12	12
23	9	9	10	10	10	11	11	11	12	12	12	13
24	9	10	10	10	11	11	11	12	12	12	13	13
25	10	10	10	11	11	11	12	12	12	13	13	13
26	10	10	11	11	11	12	12	12	13	13	13	14
27	10	11	11	11	12	12	12	13	13	13	14	14
28	11	11	11	12	12	12	13	13	13	14	14	14
29	11	11	12	12	12	13	13	13	14	14	14	15
30	11	12	12	12	13	13	13	14	14	14	15	15
31	12	12	12	13	13	13	14	14	14	15	15	15
32	12	12	13	13	13	14	14	14	15	15	15	16
33	12	13	13	13	14	14	14	15	15	15	16	16
34	13	13	13	14	14	14	15	15	15	16	16	16
35	13	13	14	14	14	15	15	15	16	16	16	17
36	13	14	14	14	15	15	15	16	16	16	17	17
37	14	14	14	15	15	15	16	16	16	17	17	17
38	14	14	15	15	15	16	16	16	17	17	17	18
39	14	15	15	15	16	16	16	17	17	17	18	18
40	15	15	15	16	16	16	17	17	17	18	18	18
41	15	15	16	16	16	17	17	17	18	18	18	19
42	15	16	16	16	17	17	17	18	18	18	19	19
43	16	16	16	17	17	17	18	18	18	19	19	19
44	16	16	17	17	17	18	18	18	19	19	19	20
45	16	17	17	17	18	18	18	19	19	19	20	20
46	17	17	17	18	18	18	19	19	19	20	20	20
47	17	17	18	18	18	19	19	19	20	20	20	21
48	17	18	18	18	19	19	19	20	20	20	21	21
49	18	18	18	19	19	19	20	20	20	21	21	21
50	18	18	19	19	19	20	20	20	21	21	21	22
51	18	19	19	19	20	20	20	21	21	21	22	22
52	19	19	19	20	20	20	21	21	21	22	22	22
53	19	19	20	20	20	21	21	21	22	22	22	23
54	19	20	20	20	21	21	21	22	22	22	23	23
55	20	20	20	21	21	21	22	22	22	23	23	23
56	20	20	21	21	21	22	22	22	23	23	23	24
57	20	21	21	21	22	22	22	23	23	23	24	24
58	21	21	21	22	22	22	23	23	23	24	24	24
59	21	21	22	22	22	23	23	23	24	24	24	25
60	21	22	22	22	23	23	23	24	24	24	25	25

APPENDIX 3
Instructions for Making Worksheets,
Games/Quizzes (STAD and TGT)

Making curriculum materials for STAD or TGT is very much like making worksheets and quizzes for any instructional unit. In fact, you may use any worksheets and quizzes you already have, or you may take items from other sources instead of creating entirely new worksheets and quizzes.

To make materials for STAD or TGT, follow these steps:

1. Make a Worksheet and a Worksheet Answer Sheet for each unit. A worksheet is usually a series of items that provides students with practice and self-assessment that will directly help them prepare for the quiz (STAD) or game (TGT) to follow. The number of worksheet items depends on the kind of material you are teaching. Short-answer items, such as irregular verb tenses, multiplication facts, or multiple-choice questions, probably require a longer worksheet than a unit in which each item takes longer to do, as in a long division unit. The Johns Hopkins Team Learning Project curriculum materials always use 30-item worksheets, but it is not necessary to make that exact number of items. Also, note that a set of items is not the only possible kind of worksheet. For example, in a geography unit students can fill in country names on a blank map, and in a math facts or spelling unit they can use flashcards instead of a worksheet. The main idea is to be sure that the worksheet provides *direct* practice for the quiz or game. For example, a crossword puzzle may give students some help with a spelling test, but it does not give them the kind of drill and practice that will enable them to master the spelling words. Thus, a crossword puzzle can be used as a supplementary activity, but it should not be used to replace a worksheet or flash cards that directly prepare students for a spelling test.

As soon as you have made a worksheet, also make a worksheet answer sheet. Students will use this answer sheet to check themselves as they study.

2. Make a Game/Quiz and a Game/Quiz Answer Sheet for each unit. The same sheet serves as a game in TGT and a quiz in STAD. The items on this sheet should closely parallel those on the worksheet. Develop the worksheet and the game/quiz at the same time, making each worksheet item parallel to each corresponding game/quiz item. The following are examples of parallel items:

Worksheet	Game/Quiz
1. $\frac{1}{2} + \frac{1}{2} =$	1. $1/3 + 1/3 =$

2. The car crept _____ up the hill.
   a. slow
   b. slowly
	2. Even though he was nervous, he got a
	   _____ score on the test.
	    a. good
	    b. well

3. A combination of hydrogen and flourine would be written . . .
   a. H_2F
   b. HF
   c. HF_2
   d. H_2F_2
	3. A combination of calcium and chlorine would be written . . .
	   a. Ca_2Cl
	   b. $CaCl$
	   c. $CaCl_2$
	   d. Ca_2Cl_2

4. The capital of Canada is _____.	4. The capital of Canada is _____.

Note that in questions 1 to 3, the parallel items test the same skill or concept (addition of simple fractions with like denominators, correct use of adjectives/adverbs, writing chemical formulas with elements of different valences), but they are different items. This avoids the possibility of students memorizing the *items* instead of learning the *concepts*. In item 4, however, the task is to memorize capitals of countries. Thus it is appropriate to give the same item twice, and it would of course be unfair to have a capital on the game/quiz that did not appear on the worksheet.

The number of items on the game/quiz should ordinarily be 30. This corresponds to the number of cards used in TGT or to the number used as the basis of the individual improvement score system in STAD. However, you may use shorter or longer games/quizzes if you wish. For TGT, to use any number of items up to 30, have students remove number cards for which there are no items. For STAD, use quizzes with a number of items that divides evenly into 30. For example, for a 15-item quiz, give two points for each correct answer.

For TGT, you will need to make a game/quiz answer sheet so that students can check themselves during the game. For STAD, you will need a correction key. If students correct each other's papers, you can place the answers on an overhead projector sheet or on a large piece of paper to show the class, or simply read the answers to students for correction.

A representative unit (worksheet, worksheet answers, game/quiz, and game/quiz answers) follows.

Student Team Learning

Subject: Mathematics

Worksheet: R-7   Subtraction of Three Digit Numbers

Topics: - subtracting three digits with renaming
         - word problems

Subtract

1.   574
  - 297
	6. 666
	  -148
		11. 804
		  - 425
			16. 249
			  - 168

2.   847
  - 658
	7. 743
	  - 267
		12. 628
		  -447
			17. 463
			  -276

3.   902
  - 627
	8. 426
	  -148
		13. 507
		  -318
			18. 912
			  - 655

4.   733
  - 286
	9. 525
	  - 437
		14. 624
		  - 368
			19. 647
			  - 152

5.   655
  - 257
	10. 917
	  - 648
		15. 501
		  - 287
			20. 431
			  - 265

Worksheet: R-7 Subtraction of Three Digit Numbers

Subject: Mathematics

---

21. 723
    − 546

22. 823
    − 568

23. 814
    − 657

24. 734
    − 376

25. 642
    − 286

Solve the word problems.

26. There are 990 coins on the table. Bob takes 648 of them. How many coins are left?

27. There are 502 balloons. 249 of them are blue. How many balloons are not blue?

28. In a box there are 308 apples. Jane takes 198 of them. How many apples are left in the box?

29. There are 503 children in the school. There are 246 boys. How many girls are there?

30. There are 432 crayons. Jackie broke 243 of them. How many crayons are unbroken?

Worksheet Answers
Subject: Mathematics

R-7 Subtraction of Three Digit Numbers

1.	277		16.	81
2.	189		17.	187
3.	275		18.	257
4.	447		19.	495
5.	398		20.	166
6.	518		21.	177
7.	476		22.	255
8.	278		23.	157
9.	88		24.	358
10.	269		25.	356
11.	379		26.	342 coins
12.	181		27.	253 balloons
13.	189		28.	110 apples
14.	256		29.	257 girls
15.	214		30.	189 crayons

Student Team Learning

Subject: Mathematics

Game/Quiz: R-7   Subtraction of Three Digit Numbers

Subtract

1. 735
    − 278

2. 465
    − 386

3. 957
    − 648

4. 803
    − 627

5. 655
    − 347

6. 777
    − 188

7. 734
    − 376

8. 516
    − 245

9. 626
    − 447

10. 818
    − 520

11. 404
    − 116

12. 737
    − 609

13. 402
    − 138

14. 456
    − 398

15. 812
    − 566

16. 307
    − 75

17. 724
    − 567

18. 624
    − 395

19. 647
    − 152

20. 431
    − 265

Subject: Mathematics

---

21.   515
     - 369

22.   991
     - 709

23.   502
     - 369

24.   423
     - 245

25.   872
     - 516

Solve the word problems

26. There are 112 balls in the gym. 88 are flat. How many ball are not flat?

27. There are 409 pencils. 22 are red pencils. How many pencils are not red?

28. Jim has 931 candy bars. He gives away 646 of them. How many candy bars does he keep?

29. There are 871 doors in the hotel. 575 are closed. How many doors are open?

30. There are 1000 papers on the floors. Jack picks up 827 of them. How many papers are still on the floor?

Game/Quiz Answers

Subject: Mathematics

R-7   Subtraction of Three Digit Numbers

1.	457	16.	232
2.	79	17.	157
3.	309	18.	229
4.	176	19.	495
5.	308	20.	166
6.	589	21.	146
7.	358	22.	282
8.	271	23.	133
9.	179	24.	178
10.	298	25.	356
11.	288	26.	24 balls
12.	128	27.	387 pencils
13.	264	28.	285 candy bars
14.	58	29.	296 doors
15.	246	30.	173 papers

APPENDIX 4
Sample Jigsaw II Unit

This appendix contains a complete Jigsaw II Unit. It is based on the Introduction to this publication for the sake of illustration. Before using Jigsaw II, you might use this unit with other teachers to get a student's-eye view of the technique.

The expert sheet appears below. If you are simulating Jigsaw II, assign yourself to a team, pick one of the four topics and then reread the Introduction. Then discuss the topic with your "expert group," return to your team to report on your topic, and take the quiz. The quiz answers are as follows: *c b a b a c d d.*

Expert Sheet

To read: The Introduction to this publication

Topics: 1. What are the principal features of STAD, TGT, and Jigsaw?
         2. What has the research on Student Team Learning found?
         3. Why do the Student Team Learning techniques produce the effects that they do?
         4. What are some of the reasons that teachers might adopt one of the Student Team Learning techniques?

Quiz: Student Team Learning

1a. What is the main difference between STAD and TGT?
    (a) STAD is less expensive to use than TGT.
    (b) STAD is used mostly in social studies, TGT in mathematics and language arts.
    (c) STAD uses quizzes, TGT uses instructional games.
    (d) STAD uses practice worksheets, TGT does not.

1b. What do TGT and Jigsaw have in common?
    (a) Expert groups
    (b) Heterogeneous teams
    (c) Quizzes
    (d) Instructional games

2a. Which of the Student Team Learning techniques has been evaluated in the largest number of studies?
    (a) TGT
    (b) STAD
    (c) Jigsaw

2b. Which of the following is the most consistent finding for all Student Team Learning techniques?
    (a) Improved attitudes
    (b) Improved intergroup relations
    (c) Increased self-esteem
    (d) Increased satisfaction

3a. Which of the following is a reason implied in the Introduction for the effects of team techniques on learning?

(a) Peer support for academic performance
(b) Effectiveness of peer tutoring
(c) Increased mutual concern
(d) Improved student attitudes

3b. Which is *not* a reason implied in the Introduction for the effects of Student Team Learning on positive intergroup relations?
(a) Students in multiethnic teams must interact.
(b) Teams in general increase mutual concern among teammates.
(c) Students in multiethnic teams learn about each other's cultures.
(d) Students in multiethnic teams learn to help each other.

4a. Which is *not* a reason that a teacher might adopt Student Team Learning techniques?
(a) Team techniques allow the teacher to be a facilitator rather than a director.
(b) Team techniques improve student learning, positive intergroup relations, and other dimensions.
(c) Team techniques provide an effective classroom management system.
(d) Team techniques take less time than traditional techniques.

4b. Which traditional classroom activity do STAD and TGT replace most effectively?
(a) Teacher lectures
(b) Supplementary activities
(c) Homework
(d) Drill

APPENDIX 5
Sample Record Forms

TEAM SUMMARY SHEET

Team Name _____

Team Members	1	2	3	4	5	6	7	8	9	10	11	12	13	14
Total Team Score														
Transformed Team Score														
Team Standing This Week														
Cumulative Score														
Cumulative Standing														

QUIZ SCORE SHEET (STAD and Jigsaw II)

Student	Date: Quiz: Base Score	Quiz Score	Improvement Points	Date: Quiz: Base Score	Quiz Score	Improvement Points	Date: Quiz: Base Score	Quiz Score	Improvement Points

TOURNAMENT TABLE ASSIGNMENT SHEET (TGT)

Tournament Number:

Student	Team	1	2	3	4	5	6	7	8	9	10	11	12	13

TABLE #_____ GAME SCORE SHEET (TGT) ROUND #_____

PLAYER	TEAM	Game 1	Game 2	Game 3	DAY'S TOTAL	TOURNAMENT POINTS

TABLE #_____ GAME SCORE SHEET (TGT) ROUND #_____

PLAYER	TEAM	Game 1	Game 2	Game 3	DAY'S TOTAL	TOURNAMENT POINTS

TABLE #_____ GAME SCORE SHEET (TGT) ROUND #_____

PLAYER	TEAM	Game 1	Game 2	Game 3	DAY'S TOTAL	TOURNAMENT POINTS

TABLE #_____ GAME SCORE SHEET (TGT) ROUND #_____

PLAYER	TEAM	Game 1	Game 2	Game 3	DAY'S TOTAL	TOURNAMENT POINTS

Bibliography

1. Aronson, E. *The Jigsaw Classroom*. Beverly Hills, Calif.: Sage, 1978.

2. Ballard, M.; Corman, L.; Gottlieb, J.; and Kaufman, M. "Improving the Social Status of Mainstreamed Retarded Children." *Journal of Educational Psychology* 69 (1977): 605–11.

3. Blaney, N. T.; Stephan, S.; Rosenfield, D.; Aronson, E.; and Sikes, J. "Interdependence in the Classroom: A Field Study." *Journal of Educational Psychology* 69, no. 2 (1977): 121–28.

4. Bronfenbrenner, U. *Two Worlds of Childhood*. New York: Russell Sage Foundation, 1970.

5. Coleman, J. S. *The Adolescent Society*. New York: Free Press of Glencoe, 1961

6. Cooper, L.; Johnson, D. W.; Johnson, R.; and Wilderson, F. "Effects of Cooperative, Competitive, and Individualistic Experiences on Interpersonal Attraction Among Heterogeneous Peers." *Journal of Social Psychology* 111 (1980): 243–52.

7. DeVries, D. L.; Edwards, K. J.; and Slavin, R. E. "Biracial Learning Teams and Race Relations in the Classroom: Four Field Experiments on Teams-Games-Tournament." *Journal of Educational Psychology* 70 (1978): 356–62.

8. DeVries, D. L.; Lucasse, P.; and Shackman, S. "Small Group Versus Individualized Instruction: A Field Test of Their Relative Effectiveness." Paper presented at Annual Convention of American Psychological Association, New York, 1979.

9. DeVries, D. L., and Slavin, R. E. "Teams-Games-Tournament (TGT): Review of Ten Classroom Experiments." *Journal of Research and Development in Education* 12 (1978): 28–38.

10. Gerard, H. B., and Miller, N. *School Desegregation: A Long-Range Study*. New York: Plenum Press, 1975.

11. Gonzales, A. "Classroom Cooperation and Ethnic Balance." Paper presented at Annual Convention of American Psychological Association, New York, 1979.

12. Good, T., and Grouws, D. "The Missouri Mathematics Effectiveness Project: An Experimental Study in Fourth Grade Classrooms." *Journal of Educational Psychology* 71 (1979): 355–62.

13. Janke, R. "The Teams-Games-Tournament (TGT) Method and the Behavioral Adjustment and Academic Achievement of Emotionally Impaired Adolescents." Paper presented at Annual Convention of American Educational Research Association, Toronto, 1978.

14. Lucker, G. W.; Rosenfield, D.; Sikes, J.; and Aronson, E. "Performance in the Interdependent Classroom: A Field Study." *American Educational Research Journal* 13 (1976): 115-23.

15. Madden, N. A., and Slavin, R. E. "Cooperative Learning and Social Acceptance of Mainstreamed Academically Handicapped Students." *Journal of Special Education* 17 (1983): 171-82.

16. Sharan, S., and Sharan, Y. *Small-Group Teaching*. Englewood Cliffs, N.J.: Educational Technology Publications, 1976.

17. Slavin, R. E. "Classroom Reward Structure: An Analytic and Practical Review." *Review of Educational Research* 47, no. 4 (1977): 633-50.

18. _____. *Student Learning Team Techniques: Narrowing the Achievement Gap Between the Races*. Baltimore: Center for Social Organization of Schools, Johns Hopkins University, 1977. Report No. 228.

19. _____. "A Student Team Approach to Teaching Adolescents with Special Emotional and Behavioral Needs." *Psychology in the Schools* 14, no. 1 (1977): 77-84.

20. _____. "Student Teams and Achievement Divisions." *Journal of Research and Development in Education* 12 (1978): 39-49.

21. _____. "Effects of Biracial Learning Teams on Cross-Racial Friendships." *Journal of Educational Psychology* 71 (1979): 381-87.

22. _____. *Using Student Team Learning*. 3d ed. Baltimore: Center for Social Organization of Schools, Johns Hopkins University, 1986.

23. _____. "Effects of Individual Learning Expectations on Student Achievement." *Journal of Educational Psychology* 72 (1980): 520-24.

24. _____. *Cooperative Learning*. New York: Longman, 1983.

25. _____. *Cooperative Learning: Student Teams*. 2d ed. Washington, D.C.: National Education Association, 1987.

26. Slavin, R. E., and Karweit, N. "Cognitive and Affective Outcomes of an Intensive Student Team Learning Experience." *Journal of Experimental Education* 50 (1981): 29-35.

27. Slavin, R. E.; Leavey, M.; and Madden, N. A. "Effects of Student Teams and Individualized Instruction on Student Mathematics Achievement, Attitudes, and Behaviors." Paper presented at Annual Convention of American Educational Research Association, New York, 1982.

28. Slavin, R. E., and Oickle, E. "Effects of Cooperative Learning Teams on Student Achievement and Race Relations: Treatment by Race Interactions." *Sociology of Education* 54 (1981): 174-80.

29. Ziegler, S. "The Effectiveness of Cooperative Learning Teams for Increasing Cross-Ethnic Friendship: Additional Evidence." *Human Organization* 40 (1981): 264-68.

Additional Resources
for the Second Edition

A. Madden, N., and Slavin, R. E. "Mainstreaming Students with Mild Handicaps: Academic and Social Outcomes." *Review of Educational Research* 53 (1983): 519–69.

B. Slavin, R. E. "When Does Cooperative Learning Increase Student Achievement?" *Psychological Bulletin* 94 (1983): 429–45.

C. Slavin, R. E. "Team Assisted Individualization: Cooperative Learning and Individualized Instruction in the Mainstreamed Classroom." *Remedial and Special Education* 5, no. 6 (1984): 33–42.

D. Slavin, R. E. "Cooperative Learning: Applying Contact Theory in Desegregated Schools." *Journal of Social Issues* 41, no. 3 (1985): 45–62.

E. Slavin, R. E. "Team Assisted Individualization: A Cooperative Learning Solution for Adaptive Instruction in Mathematics." In *Adapting Instruction to Individual Differences*, edited by M. Wang and H. Walberg, pp. 236–53. Berkeley, Calif.: McCutchan, 1985.

F. Slavin R. E. *Educational Psychology: Theory into Practice*. Englewood Cliffs, N.J.: Prentice-Hall, 1986.

G. Slavin, R. E. "Combining Cooperative Learning and Individualized Instruction." *Arithmetic Teacher* 35, no. 3 (1987): 14–16.

H. Slavin, R. E. "Cooperative Learning and the Cooperative School." *Educational Leadership* 45, no. 3 (1987): 7–13.

I. Slavin, R. E., and Karweit, N. "Mastery Learning and Student Teams: A Factorial Experiment in Urban General Mathematics Classes." *American Educational Research Journal* 21 (1984): 725–36.

J. Slavin, R. E., and Karweit, N. L. "Effects of Whole-Class, Ability-Grouped, and Individualized Instruction on Mathematics Achievement." *American Educational Research Journal* 22 (1985): 351–67.

K. Slavin, R. E.; Leavey, M.; and Madden, N. A. "Combining Cooperative Learning and Individualized Instruction: Effects on Student Mathematics Achievement, Attitudes, and Behaviors." *Elementary School Journal* 84 (1984): 409–22.

L. Slavin, R. E.; Leavey, M. B.; and Madden, N. A. *Team Accelerated Instruction—Mathematics*. Watertown, Mass.: Mastery Education Corporation, 1985.

M. Slavin, R. E.; Madden, N. A.; and Leavey, M. "Effects of Team Assisted Individualization on the Mathematics Achievement of Academically Handicapped and Nonhandicapped Students." *Journal of Educational Psychology* 76 (1984): 813–19.

N. Slavin, R. E., and others, eds. *Learning to Cooperate, Cooperating to Learn.* New York: Plenum, 1985.

O. Stevens, R. J.; Madden, N. A.; Slavin, R. E.; and Farnish, A. M. "Cooperative Integrated Reading and Composition: Two Field Experiments." *Reading Research Quarterly* 22 (1987): 433–54.

WESTMAR COLLEGE LIBRARY

LB 1032 .S546 1988
Slavin, Robert E.
Student team learning
          (89-842)

DEMCO